CRISIS AND CHAOS:
LIFE WITH THE COMBAT VETERAN
The Stories of Families Living and Coping with
Posttraumatic Stress Disorder (PTSD)

Colleen McCarty-Gould

1998. 189 pages. ISBN 1-56072-617-2. $18.95.

Posttraumatic Stress Disorder is marked by symptoms following exposure to extreme trauma. For loved ones of combat veterans unable to shake the grip of war, the homefront is indeed a battlefield. For many families, the memories of the departure, and all the plans and hopes for tomorrow, are shattered when the loved one returns. He comes home, but he's different. He returns from that faraway place, but yet a part of him seems to be there still, thousands of miles away. For centuries societies have shipped their youth off to war, fully expecting them to return home the same, to pick up where they left off, to carry on and to "fit in."

Though this extraordinary book focuses on the uniqueness of war and PTSD, the disorder is also associated with other large-scale traumas like natural disasters and personal traumas like rape, sexual abuse and domestic violence. Although the severity of the veteran's trauma, and therefore the effects of that trauma vary from home to home, certainly one principle universally applies: Young people who see or participate in the atrocities of combat do not come out of the experience unscathed. This unique book brings their plight home.

CONTENTS:

CRISIS AND CHAOS: LIFE WITH THE COMBAT VETERAN

Gentlepeople: Please send_____copies. Payment enclosed_____Send Proforma Invoice_____
(New York State residents please add appropriate sales tax)

Credit Card number_____Expiration Date____(Mo)____(Yr)

Please charge to my credit card: Type of Credit Card_____

Authorized Signature_____

Name:_____

Address_____

Kroshka Books
An Imprint of Nova Science Publishers
6080 Jericho Turnpike, Suite 207
Commack, New York 11725
Tel. (516)-499-3103   Fax (516)-499-3146   E-mail: Novascience@Earthlink.net
http:// www.nexusworld.com/nova

CRISIS AND CHAOS:
LIFE WITH THE COMBAT VETERAN

THE STORIES OF FAMILIES LIVING AND COPING
WITH POST-TRAUMATIC STRESS DISORDER
(PTSD)

CRISIS AND CHAOS:
LIFE WITH THE COMBAT VETERAN

THE STORIES OF FAMILIES LIVING AND COPING WITH POST-TRAUMATIC STRESS DISORDER (PTSD)

COLLEEN MCCARTY-GOULD

Dear Peg,
thanks for the
friendship and
support.
Colleen McCarty-Gould
12/8/98

Kroshka Books
Commack, New York

Editorial Production: Susan Boriotti
Office Manager: Annette Hellinger
Graphics: Frank Grucci and John T'Lustachowski
Information Editor: Tatiana Shohov
Book Production: Donna Dennis, Patrick Davin, Christine Mathosian, Tammy Sauter and Diane Sharp
Circulation: Maryanne Schmidt
Marketing/Sales: Cathy DeGregory

Library of Congress Cataloging-in-Publication Data

McCarty-Gould, Colleen.
    Crisis and chaos : life with the combat veteran : the stories of families living and coping with post-traumatic stress disorder (PTSD) / Colleen McCarty-Gould.
        p.   cm.
    ISBN 1-56072-617-2
    1. Post-traumatic stress disorder--Patients--Family relationships. 2. Veterans--Mental health. I. Title.
RC552.P67M385   1998   98-34038
616.85'21—dc21   CIP

Copyright © 1998 by Colleen McCarty-Gould
    Kroshka Books, a division of
    Nova Science Publishers, Inc.
    6080 Jericho Turnpike, Suite 207
    Commack, New York 11725
    Tele. 516-499-3103   Fax 516-499-3146
    e-mail: Novascience@earthlink.net
    e-mail: Novascil@aol.com
    Web Site: http://www.nexusworld.com/nova

Printed in the United States of America

CONTENTS

AUTHOR'S NOTE

For simplicity, veterans are referred to as "he" throughout this book despite the fact that many veterans are female. The author begs for reader understanding regarding the need to keep references brief and simple; she does not intend to offend female veterans, who have long played a significant role in the military.

Because female veterans also suffer from Posttraumatic Stress Disorder, information contained in this book applies to them and their male counterparts. In addition, Chapter 13 showcases the stories of female veterans with PTSD and those who love them.

To protect the privacy (and in some cases the safety) of persons interviewed, all names and identifying features have been changed.

ACKNOWLEDGMENTS

The author extends grateful acknowledgment for permission to use excerpts from the following copyrighted works:

The American Legion. Reprinted with permission of The American Legion, 5561 W. 74th St., Indianapolis, IN 46268. Several issues are cited.

American Psychiatric Association: Diagnostic and Statistical Manual of Mental Disorders, Fourth Edition. Washington, D.C., American Psychiatric Association, 1994.

Anxiety Disorders, pamphlet of the American Psychiatric Association, Washington, D.C. Copyright 1988 American Psychiatric Association.

DAV Magazine. Reprinted with permission of the Disabled American Veterans, Editorial Office, 807 Maine Ave. SW, Washington, D.C. 20024.

I Can't Get Over It, A Handbook for Trauma Survivors, by Aphrodite Matsakis, Ph.D. Copyright 1992 by Aphrodite Matsakis. Reprinted with permission of Dr. Matsakis and New Harbinger Publications.

Making Peace with Your Past: Nam Vet, by Chuck Dean. Copyright 1988, 1990 by Chuck Dean. Reprinted with permission of Chuck Dean and Multnomah Books, Questar Publishers.

National Veterans Guide, by the National Vietnam Veterans Coalition Foundation, Washington, D.C. No copyright date cited; reprinted with permission of the Board of Directors of the National Vietnam Veterans Coalition Foundation.

Readjustment Problems Among Vietnam Veterans, by Jim Goodwin. Reprinted with permission of the Disabled American Veterans, Editorial Office, 807 Main Ave. SW, Washington, D.C. 20024.

Recovering from the War, A Women's Guide to Helping Your Vietnam Vet, Your Family and Yourself, by Patience H. C. Mason. Copyright 1990 by Patience H. C. Mason. Reprinted with permission of Patience H. C. Mason.

"Road to Recovery, Posttraumatic Stress Disorder: The Hidden Victim," by Donald A. Bille, Ph.D., RN. Article in the *Journal of Psychosocial*

Nursing, Volume 31, Number 9 (1993). Reprinted with permission of Donald A. Bille and *Journal of Psychosocial Nursing.*

"Some Healthy Ways to Deal with Stress," by Abbott Northwestern Hospital, Minneapolis, Minnesota (no date). Reprinted with permission of Abbott Northwestern Hospital.

Vietnam Wives; Women and Children Surviving Life with Veterans Suffering Posttraumatic Stress Disorder, by Aphrodite Matsakis, Ph.D. Copyright 1988 by Aphrodite Matsakis. Reprinted with permission of Dr. Matsakis and Woodbine House.

The author extends grateful appreciation to the following persons, who gave so generously of their time and expertise through personal interviews for this book:

Dr. Stephen Barton, M.D., VA Hospital, Minneapolis, Minnesota

Ms. Kathryn R. Berg, M.A., L.I.C.S.W., P.A., Mendota Heights, Minnesota

Dr. Arthur S. Blank, Jr., M.D., former National Director of VA Hospital, Minneapolis, Minnesota (1982-1994)

Mr. Fred Gusman, M.S.W., National Center for PTSD, Menlo Park, California

Dr. Aphrodite Matsakis, Ph.D., Vietnam Veterans' Outreach Center, Silver Springs, Maryland

The author extends a special and warm "thank-you" to each person who agreed to be interviewed for this book, and to family and friends for their support of this project.

ABOUT THE AUTHOR

Colleen McCarty-Gould is a communications coordinator for one of Minnesota's largest school districts. She holds bachelor's degrees in German and journalism from the University of Minnesota and a master's degree in community education from St. Thomas University in St. Paul, Minnesota.

Crisis and Chaos is a labor of intense love for Colleen, whose husband is a Vietnam combat veteran with a 100 percent disability rating from Posttraumatic Stress Disorder. She and her husband are members of the Vietnam Veterans of America, Inc., Chapter 492 in Dakota County, Minnesota, to which proceeds from the sale of this book will be donated.

Colleen lives in Rosemount, Minnesota, along with her husband, Dale, and two "kids" – Charlie Brown, a buff cocker spaniel, and Tony, a maltese.

WHAT IN THE H---
IS POSTTRAUMATIC STRESS DISORDER?

PTSD AND THE EXPERTS

Dear Journal,

The journey has been long. From the pain of discovering my husband's war trauma to learning how to cope with it, I've learned so much along the way. Hopefully, some of what I've learned will help others.

To the spouse, child, parent – this book is dedicated to those who have helped our country's warriors to face the pain of their past, to mourn and to heal. You have suffered terribly on the homefront. For your unselfish love and care, you, too, are deserving of the purple heart.

There is hope for the veteran, and there is hope for those who love him. Life can be a series of wonderful tomorrows.

Colleen

FITTING IN – NO MORE

The sweet kiss of a lover ... the youthful freshness of a son or daughter ... the courage of an older brother or sister – these are among the memories of family members, waving their loved ones off to war.

For many families, the memories of the departure, and all the plans and hopes for tomorrow, are shattered when the loved one returns. He comes home, but he's different. He returns from that faraway place, but yet a part of him seems to be there still, thousands of miles away.

For centuries, societies have shipped their youth off to war, fully expecting them to return home the same. Fully expecting them to pick up where they left off, to carry on and to "fit in."

For combat veterans of all wars, the "fitting in" may not be so simple. The traumas of war – the sheer horror and surrealism – alter them forever. For a large percentage, "fitting in" becomes impossible; they spend the rest of their lives fighting the demons of war and carrying the battle to the homefront.

For loved ones of combat veterans unable to shake the grip of war, the homefront is indeed a battlefield. Though the severity of the veteran's trauma, and therefore the effects of that trauma, vary from home to home, certainly one principle universally applies: Young people who see or participate in the atrocities of combat do not come out of the experience unscathed. In some way, large or small, they are different. In some way, their belief in the goodness of mankind is darkened. In some way, their future course is forever altered.

LABELING THE AFTERMATH

Combat veterans and their loved ones have long shared the truth and secret about war: That it changes people and it changes their lives.

Well, here I am in my eighth month. Nothing has changed, except me! I only hope God will bring me back to the same Bill that left last summer. Please God, make it so when I get back people will still like me, 'cause I've really changed "too much." Don't make me like my brother Jeff. Not that he's bad. But sometimes he gets carried away. I feel like I'm like that now. Thanks.
– Entry in Bill's journal, January 1971, Bien Hoa, South Vietnam

Despite the veteran's intimate knowledge about the effects of war, the rest of the world has only recently caught on to the truth. It wasn't until 1980 that the American Psychiatric Association officially labeled the symptoms and behaviors often following trauma as Posttraumatic Stress Disorder, popularly known as "PTSD." (Experts caution that PTSD is not the only possible reaction to trauma.) Besides giving it a real name with real symptoms, the association placed the disorder alongside the other anxiety disorders, a place where it proudly stands to this day.

The real tragedy of this johnny-come-lately diagnosis, of course, is that PTSD has been around for centuries, wreaking havoc on its victims and stressing communities around the world. Sure, it hasn't had the fine label of "PTSD" for very long. But its devastation has been noted as far back as the ancient Greeks and Romans.

PTSD-type symptoms have been called many things throughout American history alone. During the Civil War, doctors and others called it "irritable heart" because of the victim's heart palpitations and chest pain. It was also known as "nostalgia" during that war because of the sufferer's intense desire to go home. But it wasn't until World War I that the symptoms, by now known as "shell shock," were said to be actually caused by the combat experience itself.[1] Shortly after World War I, renowned German therapist Sigmund Freud helped showcase the symptoms and traumas of "war neurosis." Freud also encouraged war trauma victims to engage in what he called "psychotherapy," or talking about their traumas.

During World War II, doctors continued to recognize psychological problems due to combat. By the time of the Korean War, they discovered another important key to the mystery of PTSD: Soldiers must be treated immediately after trauma to "reduce or prevent long-term traumas."[2]

And then along came Vietnam with all its mysteries and inconsistencies. Despite the horrific nature of the conflict, psychological casualties during that war actually decreased when compared to previous wars.[3] What the experts didn't realize, however, was that the Vietnam veteran was stuffing his feelings away. Stuffing them away for another day, another time and another place.

Vietnam, like World War I, created what has been coined a "lost generation," an entire crop of young people doomed to fight the ghost of war forever.

The biggest mystery surrounding PTSD is not the nature of the disorder, but the length of time – many lifetimes over – it has taken researchers, therapists and other "experts" to label and describe it. For centuries, war veterans and their loved ones have had their own private description and label for it.

Hell.

PTSD DEFINED

Posttraumatic Stress Disorder is marked by symptoms following exposure to extreme trauma. Specific criteria for diagnosis of PTSD appear in the *Diagnostic and Statistical Manual of Mental Disorders, Fourth Edition,* published by the American Psychiatric Association as the handbook for clinicians. The complete criteria for diagnosis of PTSD appear in the appendix of this book.

The diagnostic features of PTSD are as follows (reprinted with permission from the *Diagnostic and Statistical Manual of Mental Disorders, Fourth Edition.* Copyright 1994 American Psychiatric Association):[4]

The essential feature of Posttraumatic Stress Disorder is the development of characteristic symptoms following exposure to an extreme traumatic stressor involving direct personal experience of an event that involves actual or threatened death or serious injury, or other threat to one's physical integrity; or witnessing an event that involves death, injury, or a threat to the physical integrity of another person; or learning about unexpected or violent death, serious harm, or threat of death or injury experienced by a family member or other close associate (Criterion A1). The person's response to the event must involve intense fear, helplessness, or horror (or in children, the response must involve disorganized or agitated behavior) (Criterion A2). The characteristic symptoms resulting from the exposure to the extreme trauma include persistent reexperiencing of the traumatic event (Criterion B), persistent avoidance of stimuli associated with the trauma and numbing of general responsiveness (Criterion C), and persistent symptoms of increased arousal (Criterion D). The full symptom picture must be present for more than one month (Criterion E), and the disturbance must cause clinically significant distress or impairment in social, occupational, or other important areas of functioning (Criterion F).

Though this book focuses on the uniqueness of war and PTSD, the disorder is also associated with other large-scale traumas like natural disasters and personal traumas like rape, sexual abuse and domestic violence. The traumas range from single events to repeated or continuous ones.

Experts are quick to point out that PTSD is not the only possible reaction to combat trauma. Among the reactions is a normal return to society. In fact, many vets who experience the most horrific of war situations do return home to assimilate nicely back into the world. Because of its devastation on victims and families, however, PTSD is the focus of this book.

Dr. Aphrodite Matsakis is clinical coordinator for the Vietnam Veterans' Outreach Center in Silver Springs, Maryland, and a leading specialist in Posttraumatic Stress Disorder. Besides her clinical work, Dr. Matsakis has written extensively on the topic. In her book, *I Can't Get Over It, a Handbook for Trauma Survivors* (New Harbinger Publications, 1992), Dr. Matsakis writes that "PTSD is an entirely normal reaction to an abnormal amount of stress .... the symptoms of PTSD are not 'in someone's head' or a play for attention. Rather, they are the aftereffects of an event or series of events severe enough to profoundly alter a person's thinking, feelings, and physical reactions."[5]

Interestingly, Dr. Matsakis continues, PTSD is only one of two "diagnoses in the entire book (*Diagnostic and Statistical Manual of Mental Disorders*) that places the origin of the symptoms on external events rather than on the individual personality."[6] What this means is that PTSD stems from events outside the person – it does not flow from a weakness or deficiency within the person.

Dr. Matsakis and other leading researchers are quick to point out that not enough PTSD studies have been conducted, particularly regarding the physiological effects of the disorder. At times, researchers and clinicians lack even the right words to describe it (due partly to the fact the U.S. has not had large-scale traumas, like war, on home soil). Because of the newness of PTSD as an "official" disorder and the infancy of related research, additional studies and books on the topic are likely to occur during the next several decades.

SYMPTOMS AND BEHAVIORS OF PTSD

What is not debatable about Posttraumatic Stress Disorder is the potential for dramatic, life-altering symptoms and behaviors, several of which are commonly associated with the disorder. (Clarification: A symptom is something a person complains of and reports; a behavior is something observable.)

Not all veterans complain of or display all the symptoms and behaviors. They may, in fact, have an assortment of them or they may not be aware of them or they may display them at different times in their lives. PTSD commonly looks and acts like this:[7]

• Lack of Feelings – Because of their intense losses in war, vets often make up their minds not to feel or love again. They may appear to be cold and uncaring. Experts refer to this as "psychic numbing."

• Alienation – Many vets go through life avoiding feelings, social contacts and relationships. They may even go so far as to avoid intimate relationships with spouses and other loved ones. They may show no interest in work, family life or other activities.

• Anger/Rage – The vet's pent-up anger and rage may come out in erratic acts of violence. The source of the anger or rage may not be clear to those around him.

• Helplessness – Vets often complain of feeling powerless over their lives, including job and destiny.

• Depression – Feelings of sadness and hopelessness are common to PTSD, but may reach suicidal levels in some vets.

• Survival Guilt – Vets who lost many comrades, especially if they perceive themselves as being responsible for death, may spend their post-war years feeling guilty about making it home when others did not.

• Panic Attacks – These attacks can seem to come from nowhere, and are marked by such symptoms as sweating, trembling, shortness of breath, chest discomfort and fear of dying.

• Sleep Disturbance and Nightmares – The disrupted sleep of many vets manifests itself in sweating, screaming and shaking.

• Intrusive Thoughts/Flashbacks – Intrusive thoughts are recurring memories of an event. They may "intrude" frequently, interrupting the vet's ability to concentrate or function. Flashbacks are intense re-experiencing of traumatic events.

• Startle Reaction – Vets often live in a constant state of alertness and hypervigilance – "on guard" at all times. They may easily startle from noise or quick movements (e.g., hitting the floor when a plane flies overhead).

• Selective Memory/Memory Impairment – Vets often complain of being forgetful. They also report forgetting major events while remembering minute details.

The lingo of PTSD also includes the following: internal and external "triggers" which, as the label suggests, set off memories of war; "anniversary," the date on which a trauma occurred, often causing great distress; and "Post," like PTSD, a shortened version of Posttraumatic Stress Disorder.

Additional PTSD symptoms and behaviors include fantasies about "getting even," poor self-image, distrust of authority figures including the government, and self-punishing patterns of behavior, e.g., substance abuse. Physical complaints may also be part of the package; for veterans with years of untreated PTSD, physical problems are probably a reality. Those problems only muddy-up an already complex disorder.

COMPLEXITIES OF PTSD

PTSD is a complex problem. It wears many shades and many disguises. It can seem to come and go. It can be an annoyance or it can be life-threatening.

The key to what makes PTSD so complex is that it actually springs from the past. Dr. Arthur Blank, Jr., psychiatrist and former National Director of the Vet Centers (1982-1994), and former National Director of the Vet Centers (1982-1994), describes PTSD as a "disruption of the present." He details the perplexing problem of witnessing present-day anger in the veteran that actually flows from his war experiences.[8]

The issue of time further complicates the picture. Experts refer to PTSD that is "acute," "chronic" or "with delayed onset." Acute refers to PTSD in which the symptoms last less than three months. Chronic refers to PTSD in which the symptoms last three months or more. Delayed onset refers to PTSD in which the symptoms appear at least six months after the trauma occurs.[9]

Regardless of when the symptoms appear and how long they last, the most complex of all is untreated PTSD. It festers under the skin, for days, months, even years. It's particularly troublesome to Vietnam vets, who suffered many years between trauma and proper diagnosis and treatment. Much of this book focuses on untreated PTSD.

There are also many degrees of PTSD. Experts use the terms "mild," "moderate" and "severe" to describe the intensity of the disorder. They also refer to "partial" or "full-blown" PTSD to describe the number of symptoms displayed in the veteran. They even differentiate between "simple" and "complex" PTSD, simple being exposure to a single trauma and complex being exposure to extreme or repeated trauma.

There is also evidence that the nature of the trauma itself helps determine the severity of PTSD. Traumas caused by humans, such as torture or rape, appear to be more devastating than those caused by natural events.[10]

Just when the vet and others around him think they have a label, PTSD changes! According to noted PTSD researcher and author John P. Wilson, Ph.D., the disorder is not static. The ever-changing nature of PTSD has been noted particularly in Vietnam veterans, who have been found to experience stages or cycles of the disorder. The stages reflect the veteran's varying abilities to appear normal, cope with life, control symptoms and emotions, and survive safely.[11]

Along with the changing face of PTSD is the possibility of other psychological problems. Many veterans battle not only PTSD, but such problems as alcoholism, Panic Disorder and Obsessive-Compulsive Disorder as well. The veteran may also have physical problems, particularly as he approaches middle age. The medical profession refers to the existence of two or more problems at the same time as "co-morbidity."

Dr. Stephen Barton is a psychiatrist at the VA Hospital in Minneapolis, Minnesota, and former PTSD Program Team Director and Medical Director. He describes the complexity of co-morbidity as the "chicken or egg?" dilemma.[12] For example, in a veteran with both PTSD and alcoholism, which came first? Did one cause the other?

And yet another complication of PTSD is that it often interferes with a person's normal adult development. Dr. Blank explains:[13]

As we go through our 20's, 30's, 40's, 50's, etc., we continue to grow and develop; we become more mature. Our values change. We become interested in children and ... committed to parenting. Our work grows, develops and changes and hopefully flourishes in some

*way so there's a pattern. Growth and development doesn't stop at the
age of 18. It keeps right on going.*

*The problem is that when people have PTSD and it goes untreated
and goes on for a long time, their development is interfered with. It's
impeded, usually in a spotty fashion; so that, for example, a person
may grow and develop as regards parenting, but not as regards work.*

Dr. Blank adds, "The veteran is not defective. The potential continues to be
there for normal adult development."

Fred Gusman, Director of the National Center for Posttraumatic Stress
Disorder, Clinical Laboratory and Education Division, in Menlo Park,
California, describes many veterans as being stuck in time. "You have to
remember," he says, "what age they were when they went into the service.
Their maturation is frozen. (They) didn't really grow up. You can look pretty
old, but not be grown up in some ways. That doesn't mean you can't be
talented, have a skill or whatever. But it also doesn't mean that you're socially
mature."[14]

Veterans themselves frequently refer to their own lives in two simple
stages: Before the war, and after the war. They commonly refer to war as the
"cataclysmic split" that broke everything in two.

And then there's the entire baggage that veterans bring to the picture
before trauma. Experts refer to a "predisposition theory," which claims that
some personalities are more inclined to develop PTSD than others. The theory
is controversial and currently unsupported by thorough research.

Perhaps Fred Gusman sums it up most accurately when he states that
everyone brings his or her background to every event in life. "When exposed
to traumas, our suitcase pops up," he says. That suitcase contains our makeup
– our childhood, our relationships, our support system, etc.[15]

And then there's the stuff that happens to vets along the way that is not
even related to PTSD. Gusman continues: "It's hard for anybody to avoid
having some kind of life stressors – divorce, death, job changes, moving from
one part of the country or from one community to another, moving from one
side of town to another. There's a variation and degree of social trauma that
occurs beyond just PTSD." Combine life's normal stresses with the disorder –
and wham! You get problems, all right. PTSD also occurs within specific
societal frameworks, within specific timeframes, countries, political settings
and economic settings.

The tricky thing facing therapists, Gusman concludes, is that the complexities of PTSD make it difficult to identify the person initially exposed to the trauma. "We're seeing the aftermath," he explains. "In order for us to get acquainted with who it really was that was exposed to those war-zone events, we have to get acquainted with who they were before; so we can understand who was affected and what the end product was, what came out of all that."[16]

THE FACES OF PTSD

Unfortunately, the horrors of war are not confined to a specific culture or time. They are universal and they date back to the days of fighting with spears, bows and arrows.

If assembled, living victims of war trauma could create legions and legions of soldiers. While the number is difficult to pinpoint, evidence shows that a large percentage of the fighting forces from each of America's wars has indeed, now or at some time, battled the demons of combat.

Most research about PTSD stems from the Vietnam War and the phenomena that occurred during that war. What surprised observers at the time was that psychological breakdowns on the battlefield actually decreased when compared to previous wars. A second surprise occurred after the war, when large numbers of veterans appeared to be affected by their combat experience.[17] Researchers noted a particularly high increase in problems in 1973, the year that America withdrew from the war. These observations were curious indeed. Many wondered why the Vietnam veteran maintained so well during the war, only to crash upon coming home.

In the years following the war, many professionals across the country noted that Vietnam veterans were not adjusting easily back into society. Among those professionals was Fred Gusman, a social worker in the Palo Alto, California, area during the 1970's. In order to work effectively with veterans, Gusman began meeting with them on their own turf, in their own neighborhoods (he noted vets wouldn't come to the hospital with a problem, and if they did, they wouldn't stay). He talked with them about "just getting along in the community, rice and beans kinds of issues, sleep, legal problems, etc."[18] Gusman eventually shared his observations about Vietnam vets with others in the field, and in 1978, began the first inpatient PTSD program in the nation. In 1988 he wrote a proposal with a team of professionals. The proposal was accepted and resulted in a multi-location National Center for PTSD.

The reasons for high PTSD casualties among Vietnam veterans are many but stem from two basic categories of problems: what happened to the veteran during the war, and what happened to him directly after the war. Combined, these periods of time make up the quirkiness of Vietnam.

As to experiences during the war, military historians and psychiatrists alike point to a system introduced in Vietnam that sent young people into war entirely alone (called "DEROS," which gave each soldier an expected date of return from overseas). The individual nature of the war contrasted greatly to World War II, famous for its cohesive units and high morale. This individual tone of the war further robbed soldiers of the necessary debriefing that occurs within units that return home together (the speed of airplane travel is also to blame, of course, for the quick return of soldiers from Vietnam).

Experts further blame confusing ideology of the war and the lack of an easily identifiable enemy, often women and children. Added to the picture is the fact that most soldiers who fought in Vietnam were barely 20 years old, far younger than those of America's other wars.[19]

What happened to the Vietnam veteran upon returning home is legendary, the stuff of books and movies. The stories of being spat upon, facing angry protesters, hearing "baby killer" at every turn are well-known contrasts to the victory parades of World War II and, and, more recently Desert Storm. Dr. Blank reinforces the criticalness of the post-Vietnam period:[20]

In my view, the situation in the 1990's as regards Vietnam veterans with PTSD is very much a result not just of the war but of what happened in the post-war period. It was a very unusual situation I think. I know that veterans of all wars have adjustment difficulties post war. I know that many of them have trouble debriefing and talking with other people about their experiences. But it seems to me that was extremely intensified in the case of Vietnam. Essentially all Vietnam veterans with PTSD got the message, "don't talk about it, we don't want to hear about it. And besides which you shouldn't have gone" or "you should have won" or "what terrible things did you do" or whatever. There were all these negative messages they got; they were very real. They got them from friends, sometimes from family. Certainly got them from the community, certainly got them from the media.

Tom is a Vietnam vet who agrees. Though his one tour in the early 1970's was nearly three decades ago, he still recalls the pain of trying to hitchhike home from California to the Midwest. "I was in uniform," he says, "and got dropped off near Berkeley, the anti-Vietnam capitol of the world." He shakes his head at the memory of not being able to get a ride home. "I had to call home to the Midwest for someone to come and get me."

Fighting in Vietnam, he concludes, is like playing in the Super Bowl. "You have the ball, you make it to the 98-yard line, and then you turn around – there's no crowd. Or the crowd is eating peanuts and doing other things ..."

Another Vietnam vet describes his ambivalent feelings over the passing of an amendment in his state to award bonuses to Gulf War vets. "I'm happy they got the bonus," he explains of his comrades of a later war. "But you better believe the public wouldn't have voted to give us guys a bonus. Hell, they'd have preferred to kick us in the teeth."

Bill, a veteran of two tours, angrily describes his stint in Vietnam. "How come no one has ever asked me what war is like?" he says. "Well, I'll tell you what it's like. War is shaking, shaking all over so your body rocks. It never stops during your whole time in-country." Today, only the man's legs shake – a lasting souvenir of war.

The actual number of Vietnam veterans battling PTSD is said to be between 480,000 and 1.5 million, with many not realizing they have it.[21] Though ignored for years, many female veterans of the war also fight PTSD. Reports vary as to the exact number of women who served and are affected by PTSD, but studies estimate that 8-11,000 women served in Vietnam, and around 20 percent of them have PTSD.[22]

PTSD extends beyond Vietnam, of course. The American Psychiatric Association describes the prevalence of PTSD in both the general and at-risk populations (reprinted with permission from the *Diagnostic and Statistical Manual of Mental Disorders, Fourth Edition.* Copyright 1994 American Psychiatric Association):[23]

Community-based studies reveal a lifetime prevalence for Posttraumatic Stress Disorder ranging from one percent to 14 percent, with the variability related to methods of ascertainment and the population sampled. Studies of at-risk individuals (e.g., combat veterans, victims of volcanic eruptions or criminal violence) have yielded prevalence rates ranging from three percent to 58 percent.

Veterans of America's other wars, before and after Vietnam, are also at risk for PTSD. "There is mounting evidence that many Korean and World War II veterans are also afflicted," writes Ken Scharnberg in *The American Legion* magazine (January 1994).[24] Patience Mason writes about World War II vets and PTSD in her book, *Recovering from the War* (Penguin Books, 1990):[25]

... World War II vets suffered, and continue to suffer, psychological changes from combat ... A veteran with enough of these changes can be diagnosed as having PTSD. Right now, delayed PTSD is striking many more World War II veterans, who adjusted well right after the war, as they retire, or lose their wives. Others of them are revealing that they have felt numb, or couldn't sleep, or had combat nightmares since they got back from the war but never told anyone.

Though data is new regarding Desert Storm, there is evidence that more than 200 veterans of that war have confirmed PTSD, and several hundred more have PTSD-type symptoms.[26]

The far-reaching grasp of PTSD is further documented in the records of the Vet Centers, which offer counseling programs for veterans of the Gulf War, Vietnam, Lebanon, Grenada and Panama. The centers are funded by the Department of Veterans Affairs with local offices throughout the country. According to an article about the centers that appeared in the April 1993 issue of *The American Legion*, "most centers report that between 75 and 80 percent of the veterans seeking help at a Vet Center suffer from combat-related psychological problems."[27]

Of the quarter million veterans who are homeless, many are believed to suffer from Posttraumatic Stress Disorder. And the thousands upon thousands of veterans who have taken their own lives are believed by professionals and family members alike to have been unable to come to peace with their war experiences. Many studies point to the startling revelation that more Vietnam veterans have died from suicide than were actually killed in battle (more than 58,000 died during the war).

The total number of PTSD victims from war is, by any modest calculation, in the millions. The final casualty lists must certainly include those who returned, but left their hearts and souls on foreign soil. As one vet puts it: "Some came back, some didn't. Some came back half-assed, like me."

CHAPTER ONE

POW's on the Homefront

PTSD AND THE FAMILY

Dear Journal,
    Don't understand why things have become so crazy around here. He's ruining my life. Wish I could get away!
    Feel scared and lonely. Worried about the kids, too. Sometimes they act just like their Dad. Wish things would get back to normal. What if they never do? Feel like a prisoner in my own home.

    Me

Topsy-Turvy Family Life

Sarah knew something was very wrong the minute she turned onto her street. The red flashing lights from the squad cars ... the ambulance parked a block away ... the police SWAT team with guns drawn. She prayed for her husband's safety but knew instantly that her worst nightmare might be unfolding.

She remembered his mood that morning. She recalled the faraway look in his eyes and the cold, cold stare. It was a look she had gotten used to over the past couple of years.

Sarah pulled into her driveway and got out of the car slowly. Several SWAT team members surrounded her and tried to escort her out of the way. But she refused.

"M'am, you've got to leave. This is a dangerous situation. We've got a man inside with guns. He says he's going to blow up the VA Hospital. Please step aside ..."

Again Sarah refused. She turned away from the officers, walked up the driveway and approached her front door. At that point, she turned to the fleet of red flashing lights and men in uniform and said calmly, "I will get my husband into the ambulance. It would be better if he didn't see all this commotion. We will be out in a minute."

Sarah's husband, Bill, was strapped into the ambulance and taken to the hospital for psychiatric evaluation. A couple of days later, the evaluation came back the same as always, the same as it had during countless similar episodes. Bill, the report said, was suffering from Posttraumatic Stress Disorder brought on by his two tours in Vietnam. The couple eventually received a copy of the report at home. Sarah filed it away along with all the others.

While dramatic, this story is not unique. Each day in homes across the country, family members and loved ones of veterans fight a subversive enemy, one they cannot see and one they cannot begin to understand. Each day is a battlefield, where the poorly equipped square off against a heavily armed foe. As Sarah explains, "I'm just a normal person trying to live a normal life. How can I be expected to know how to live with someone who says his head's going to explode? My husband has had decades to build up his PTSD. I've had no time to learn how to fight it."

For spouses and family members living with PTSD, the battles are indeed tough. They face anti-social behavior, depression, anger, abuse and even suicide. They live with the reality of isolation. They have learned to cross Christmas and birthdays off the calendar because it's too hard to celebrate them alone. And they wake up each day knowing that they may win the battle, but they have made no significant gains on the war.

Loved ones of vets with PTSD describe life in many ways – confusing, frightening, challenging, lonely, even "mind-numbing." The father of a Vietnam combat veteran, who has watched his son deteriorate over the years, describes life with PTSD as "a real roller coaster." The son of a combat vet sums up life with his father as livable, but very hard.

Unrelenting is yet another way in which life with PTSD is described. Says the spouse of a vet: "Cancer is sometimes in remission. PTSD never is."

MOUNTING CASUALTIES OF WAR

Though research is inconclusive regarding the number of loved ones affected by PTSD, everyone, experts and families alike, agree that the number is high. It is impossible, they say, not to be affected by someone battling such a horrible problem. The closer the proximity to the person with PTSD, such as the spouse, the greater the impact.

The tentacles reach further than the spouse, however. They also reach out to children; parents; extended family members including brothers, sisters, in-laws, grandparents, nieces, nephews and cousins; business associates, professional colleagues and employers; and friends and neighbors. In addition, veterans with PTSD – because they live and work in communities – also stress available social and criminal justice systems. (Some data for Vietnam veterans suggests, for example, lower-than-average wages and higher-than-average divorce rates and criminal activity.)

In her trail-blazing book, *Vietnam Wives* (Woodbine House, 1988), Dr. Aphrodite Matsakis writes: "... an estimated 900,000 Vietnam wives and partners and approximately 1,098,000 children may also be affected (by PTSD), not to mention the approximately 4.7 million members of the vet's extended family."[1]

Chuck Dean, founder and former executive director of the veterans' support organization Point Man International, uses the word "staggering" to describe the impact of the Vietnam War, both on families and on the nation. Dean writes: "The vast majority of Vietnam combat veterans have been depressed since the war. And statistics tell us that each of us (each veteran) will significantly influence and affect a minimum of five other people in our lifetime" (excerpted from the book *Making Peace with Your Past: Nam Vet*, by Chuck Dean, Multnomah Books, Questar Publishers, copyright 1988 by Chuck Dean).[2]

Point Man's Homefront Project has support chapters for spouses of veterans experiencing the "war at home." It boasts broad representation in chapters across the country.

Due to the lack of available data, it is impossible to know how many loved ones of veterans from World War II, Korea, Desert Storm and America's other conflicts are affected by PTSD. VA-sponsored family programs and private clinical practices across the country, however, actively treat family members from those wars as well.

To borrow Chuck Dean's phrase, families and communities pay a "staggering" price for war.

SECONDARY PTSD

Dorothy's son-in-law is a combat veteran who talks constantly of his war traumas. He spares no details of his bloody encounters in South Vietnam.

When Dorothy was rushed to the emergency room during a life-threatening asthma attack, she was heavily sedated and placed in the critical care unit. For days, she talked nonsensically about her blown-away arms. "I lost them," she said over and over, "in the war." When the nurses probed her curiously about which war that would be, Dorothy responded, "well, the Vietnam War, of course."

Dorothy recovered and went on to recall and share her funny story about being a war veteran – which she is not – and about being in the jungles of Southeast Asia – which she never was. She reasons that her son-in-law's stories are so vivid that she could have almost lived through them herself. (The son-in-law laughs when he tells of the far-reaching effects of his PTSD. Even the family dog is affected, he says; she suffers anxiety attacks and has to be given tranquilizers.)

Experts refer to this and the other effects of PTSD on loved ones as "secondary PTSD" or "secondary traumatization." It means that many of the veteran's symptoms and behaviors can be picked up by those around him. As Dr. Matsakis explains in *Vietnam Wives*, "One part of your family cannot suffer without that suffering affecting the entire unit."[3] Feelings of guilt, confusion, fear, anger and isolation are very common in persons living around PTSD. It is even possible for persons who hear constant war stories to actually develop combat nightmares.

However, just like PTSD differs from vet to vet, so does secondary PTSD. Loved ones bear many shades and degrees of the disorder, and no two victims suffer in the exact same way. All the complexities of PTSD itself (described in the introduction to this book) can also be present in secondary PTSD. No two vets are the same, and no two of his loved ones are the same.

Like too many vets with the disorder, many persons with secondary PTSD also do not recognize the source of their pain. As Sarah aptly puts it, "there's quite an intellectual leap from my problems to my husband's fighting in the war. Can you imagine me running to work and telling my co-workers that I feel crummy today because Bill was in the service 25 years ago?"

At the root of PTSD is the fact it is a disruption of the present stemming from the past. No wonder those living around the vet with PTSD are perplexed as to why he acts the way he does! PTSD is truly a mysterious enemy, hard to identify and hard to battle against.

Along with confusion, secondary PTSD victims frequently complain of living what the experts refer to as a "reactive lifestyle." In a reactive home, everyone reacts to the veteran's PTSD and the veteran's problems. Everyone runs around in a constant state of hyperness. Everyone tries hard to please and appease the veteran. Chuck Dean explains the futility of all this nonsense: "It's not easy trying to keep up with someone who is running fast enough to blot out his mental images of a past time of terror, pain, and a feeling of unworthiness" (excerpted from the book *Making Peace With Your Past: Nam Vet*, by Chuck Dean, Multnomah Books, Questar Publishers, copyright 1988 by Chuck Dean).[4] In the end, families just wear themselves out and get nowhere.

Life with PTSD has also been called a combat zone. "It is not an exaggeration to say that a warlike atmosphere is created in the sense that there's a lack of feeling of safety," reports Dr. Arthur Blank, Jr., psychiatrist and former National Director of the Vet Centers.[5] "It (PTSD) comes from war, which is fundamentally the situation that's dangerous and unreliable. The problem with PTSD, is that that atmosphere lives on in the mind of the veteran and it gets re-created in some fashion in the present in the home." This lack of a feeling of safety can come from many things. Perhaps Dad (or Mom) cannot handle everyday problems. Or perhaps there's drug use, weapons, violent acting-out and other real dangers in the home. Life in the combat zone means everyone "walks point." Everyone walks on eggshells. And everyone is afraid.

The real impact of PTSD on loved ones is that they focus so hard on the veteran and his problems that they too often ignore their own needs. It is not uncommon for the spouse of a vet with PTSD to miss her own doctor appointments. Or for the child to drop out of school activities to "take care of Dad." Or for the parents to give up their lifelong dream of owning a retirement home to take in the son or daughter with PTSD. In relegating their own needs and wishes, loved ones feel bitter and angry. They complain about their "lot in life." They feel like victims.

Hand-in-hand with feeling like victims is the tendency of loved ones to assert: "I'm the well one, you (the vet with PTSD) are the sick one."

Psychotherapist Kathryn Berg, who works in private practice in the Minneapolis-St. Paul area, describes the dangers of this way of thinking:[6]

> *Often spouses or partners begin to see the veteran with PTSD as the "sick one." With all their focus on the "sick one," they are not examining what their own accommodation and adjustment has done to themselves. They often feel like victims of their circumstances and begin to act much like victims – passive, helpless, hopeless, blaming others, etc.*

Finally, families living with PTSD begin to see themselves as different. They begin to view not only the veteran, but themselves, as square pegs in a round-hole society. All the trauma, all the fixation on the past – realistically, they realize that they do not live the same lives as their neighbors. Sarah describes her own feelings of being set apart from the world around her:

> *As a professional woman, I often have meetings in the evening. I usually try to stop home for a bite to eat between the regular work day and my meeting. I can't tell you the number of times when, during these quick dinners, I've had to face the rescue squad, hauling my husband away to the hospital. When I go to my meeting and face my work colleagues, I can't help but be jealous of them. They seem so calm and well-prepared. I know none of them has been through, ever, what I've been through.*

Sarah marvels at the control that others seem to have over their lives. "When one of my friends says she's going home to make dinner and watch a movie, she's able to do just that – go home, make dinner and watch a movie. When I go home, I don't know what awaits me. I don't know if I'll have a calm night or face World War III."

The specific symptoms and behaviors of PTSD and their impact on families and other loved ones are fully fleshed out in the remaining chapters of this book.

A PURPLE HEART FOR MOM

Spouses, girlfriends or boyfriends, children and others living with the vet are most impacted by his PTSD. Clinically, they are most often diagnosed with the symptoms and behaviors of secondary PTSD. They simply live too close to the veteran not to be affected.

And the effects are dramatic, say the experts. Significant others may be impacted in these ways:

• **Loss of partnership** – The vet's pulling away or inability to handle life's responsibilities may result in the partner further pulling away and even grieving over the loss of companionship. The couple's intimacy may be affected. The partner may also try to "compensate" for the vet's inability to face life – e.g., playing the role of single parent, doing all household chores, becoming the breadwinner, etc.

• **Control, Protection and Care-Giving** – Realistic or not, the partner's added responsibilities may put her in a controlling and protecting mode. She may try to control and protect the veteran and others in the household. Like the veteran, she "secures the perimeter" and takes care of everyone and everything within that perimeter. Often, the partner's over-responsibility causes time pressures.

• **Tension, Anxiety, Stress and Hyperness** – The partner may mirror the vet's tension and anxiety, or may develop those qualities from focusing too much on the vet's needs and becoming fatigued from "doing it all." The partner may also feel like life is a treadmill; she is constantly running to please the vet.

• **Anger** – The partner may harbor real anger and resentment over the situation of PTSD. Anger may be directed at the vet, the government, society at large or any other target.

• **Fear** – Partners often live in a constant state of fear because of the general milieu of anger and violence that frequently exists in households with PTSD.

• **Numbness** – Just like the vet with PTSD, the partner may shut down emotionally. The pain of PTSD overwhelms them both. It is easier not to feel anything than to feel the reality of the situation.

• **Alienation/Isolation** – The partner may not only alienate from the vet with PTSD but may alienate from the rest of the world, including others in the household, extended family members, work associates and the community at large. She may avoid social functions with a vengeance!

• **Distrust** – Like the vet, partners often distrust situations and other people. They, too, have a chip on their shoulder and a cynical attitude towards life.

• **Conflict Avoidance/Accommodation** – The partner's pleasing and appeasing of the vet results in a pattern of avoiding problems and conflicts. Partners complain of being the "buffer" between the vet and the outside world. Partners go so far as to say they also protect the outside world from the vet's behaviors.

• **Guilt/Poor Self-Esteem/Self-Doubt** – Like the vet with PTSD, partners often feel guilty for having thoughts of leaving the vet and for being unable to meet the vet's needs adequately. They often blame themselves for the situation of PTSD or doubt their own instincts about the disorder.

• **Sleeplessness** – All the stresses of PTSD may cause the partner to develop the same sleepless problems experienced by the vet. Sleep loss only feeds into the other behaviors already described.

• **Despair** – The real and imagined load of PTSD often results in the partner feeling sad, depressed or even suicidal.

Again, not all partners experience all these symptoms and behaviors. It is possible to have a combination of them in varying degrees.

CHILDREN WITH SECONDARY PTSD

Secondary PTSD affects children much differently than it affects adults. Unlike adults, children get their sense of identity from their family. Depending upon the age or stage of personal development at which they are confronted by PTSD, their sense of self is affected. Obviously, children further along in their development will not be as affected by trauma as children who are not as far along.

Imagine one's sense of self tied in with all the complexities and problems of PTSD! It is easy to see why children often mirror the problems of their parents and, sadly, the vet with PTSD Kathryn Berg elaborates:[7]

The primary function of the family is to provide for the identity development of children. With the unpredictability and the inconsistency in the family situation with PTSD, children tend not to learn to focus on their own internal development because they, too, get caught in the process of accommodation and adjustment to the disorganization.

And while they are learning to be so reactive, they're not learning a sense of themselves. They are not building their own identity. They are learning how to react to their external environment ... they are not accomplishing their own emotional developmental tasks along the way ...

So, with dysfunctioning parent(s), children tend to internalize the signals that their parent(s) are giving them. We aren't born with self-esteem, we learn it along the way and we are initially dependent upon our environment and parents to give that to us ...

There are many distinct ways in which vets with PTSD can affect their children's emotional and social development. Factors include the vet's ability to relate and get close to his children; the presence of chaos and other disruptive qualities and the relationship between the vet and his spouse. Countless variables actually make up a child's home environment.

Many vets with PTSD impair their children's social development in relating to the outside world. Viewing the world as harmful, he "sets up a perimeter" to protect his family. He may limit his family's social contacts, even limiting their comings and goings and selecting their friends. Sometimes the "perimeter" exceeds social limitations; it may go so far as to be a physical perimeter – a fence or sandbags around the yard. Regardless of whether the perimeter is controlling behavior or actual physical barriers, the result is the same. Children and other family members living within the perimeter do not develop healthy relationships with those living outside the perimeter.

Children respond to the perimeter in different ways. Fred Gusman says: "One way is to take on some of the belief systems (of the vet), the prejudices and biases. The other is to rebel against (the vet) and act out in some way. That's where you get the running away, not coming home, staying out late because (the vet) is too strange or controlling."[8]

Many children of vets with PTSD also live in the war-like atmosphere already described. Their development is further affected by the lack of safety, the sense of danger and the unreliability faced every day in the war zone. Life holds real dangers for these kids.

Many children, particularly teen-agers, take on inappropriate roles when they live with PTSD. Because Dad or Mom can't handle life, they fill in. They care for younger siblings, contribute financially, keep up the house, etc. Or they grow up too fast because, after all, they've seen it all. They become pregnant, use drugs, steal cars, quit school, quit work, pick fights, the list goes on ...

A child living with PTSD may take on the inappropriate role of being a perfectionist. He or she figures, "If I'm a star kid, then I'll get the approval of others, including the parent with PTSD." What the child does not realize, of course, is that the approval may have been forthcoming had it not been for the presence of PTSD in the family, explains Kathryn Berg, psychotherapist.[9] A child may also take on the self-perceived role of being the one who breaks up the family, adding guilt to the load. What the child can't possibly know, of course, is that the home wrecker is actually PTSD.

And sometimes children who live with PTSD try to ignore its presence altogether. Children tend not to ask questions anyway. They try to pretend PTSD doesn't exist in their family, that nothing is wrong at all. They have learned not to bring the topic up for fear of the consequences.

Unless something changes for these kids, they will bring into adulthood what they learned as children. Kathryn Berg summarizes: "All the defenses that children might learn – the people pleasing, perfectionism, care-taking, rebelling, defying, withdrawing or isolating – are then carried into adulthood even though the circumstances aren't the same any more. That's where we get emotionally arrested."[10]

OTHERS WITH SECONDARY PTSD

The tentacles of PTSD are far-reaching. Extended family members, friends and neighbors, employers and professional associates – these persons and more may be affected by the ravages of PTSD.

The closer the relationship, of course, the greater the impact. The parent who cares for the vet with PTSD is much more likely to develop secondary PTSD than the distant relative or the work colleague who keeps his professional distance. For those closely involved with the vet, the symptoms and behaviors of secondary PTSD are certainly applicable.

Common to all persons living and working around PTSD, whether closely or at a distance, is the issue of confusion. They are confused by the vet's behavior. Why is he so unpredictable? Why is he so inconsistent? Just when they think they have him figured out, he changes again!

They also feel helpless around the vet with PTSD. They wish they could cheer him up, make him feel better. Eventually, they fatigue of trying to cheer and bolster – it's just too much work. They end up judging and wondering, "Why can't he just get over it?"

Danielle's brother-in-law is a Vietnam combat vet. Though the two have a fairly distant but friendly relationship, Danielle expresses frustration at some of her brother-in-law's behaviors. She can't understand, for example, why he cancels out on family functions at the last minute. "I'm disappointed when he doesn't show up," she explains. When talking with her brother-in-law, Danielle also tries hard to avoid topics that may set him on a tailspin about Vietnam. "I'm real cautious about what I say around him," she says, alluding to an overall feeling of discomfort.

Confusing is also the way Kayla describes the behavior of her uncle, a Vietnam combat vet. During her childhood, she remembers wondering why her uncle acted the way he did. It was only at age 9-10 that she began asking serious questions about him. Now she basically understands the premise of PTSD ("He fought in the war"), but is mystified why he doesn't get any better. "Can't they (doctors) do anything about it?" she asks. Today as a young teen, Kayla is angry at the hopelessness of her uncle's situation.

In the end, many people avoid the vet with PTSD. After all, who wants to hang around someone with so many problems? Who wants to bring a downer to the party? Who wants to talk about the war all night?

It should also be pointed out that many people have these same feelings – confusion, helplessness, judging and avoidance – towards the spouse, child and others with secondary PTSD. They often criticize or make comments like: "Why don't you just leave him?" They also tire of being supportive. And they often just plain avoid the situation. In so doing, they heap more pain upon a family already hurting.

COMPLEXITIES OF SECONDARY PTSD

As with PTSD itself, secondary PTSD is very complex. There are many variables in the picture, many of which have not been fully researched.

Timing is important, for example. The spouse who marries the vet before trauma has to learn to deal with the issues of change. The spouse who meets and marries the vet after trauma may have to go through all the stages of discovery, recovery and coping. And then there's the spouse who meets and marries the vet already in the recovery and stabilization stages. There are many more possible scenarios, each lending itself to a different set of problems.

Spouses themselves fall into several categories. There are spouses who bring their own traumas, such as abuse, to the marriage. There are spouses who are dependent on the vet for his financial resources. On the other end, there are spouses who are quite independent of the vet – they have their own careers and friends. Because they have a strong sense of self and sources of support outside the marriage, they probably do not look to the vet for emotional support.

Families also fall into different categories. There are very interdependent families, in which members rely heavily on each other. At the other end, there are families in which members operate very independently and do not seek each other out for support. (Author's note: The discussion about families could fill volumes. Readers are encouraged to read other sources for complete information in this area.) As with spouses, expectations differ depending upon the type of family unit. These expectations impact how individuals and families deal with PTSD.

Add to the pot the fact that different personality types are involved, and the picture of PTSD becomes even more complicated.

Though research about PTSD is in its infancy, there are professionals in the field who believe that female spouses of vets with PTSD react differently than male spouses of vets with PTSD. In her clinical practice, psychotherapist Kathryn Berg has observed the following:[11]

In general, I see men and women (affected differently). Without sounding sexist, I would refer to traditional roles that I see men and women handling as partners of veterans with PTSD. Men who are partners of someone with PTSD tend to intensify their traditional male role. So if what they believe of themselves as men is to provide or take action about things, to solve problems intellectually, to manage/control, they will tend to do even more of that with a PTSD partner. Their adjustment and their defensive stand is going to be as captain of the ship – to take over, to manage, to fix it.

Women who are the spouses tend to take on an even more traditional role ... part of the effect on them as women and as partners, is they tend to focus even more and more on the ailing relationship.

Others in the field agree that male spouses of vets with PTSD do indeed act as captains of the ship, filling in where needed and taking care of things. Some state, however, that male spouses may not be as likely to stick around. "If it ain't workin', I'm outa here ..."

There also appear to be generational differences in the handling of PTSD, as evidenced by interviews in this book. While trauma is trauma no matter when it occurs, societal expectations of the time seem to provide a framework in which to live with and react to PTSD.

Finally, the presence of PTSD in families is further complicated by life's normal stresses and changes. Families move, have financial problems, have health problems, change and transform in all sorts of ways, independent of PTSD.

CHAPTER TWO

SOS: IS ANYBODY OUT THERE?

*PTSD AND THE CHALLENGES
OF FINDING PROPER DIAGNOSIS AND TREATMENT*

Dear Journal,
    *Well, they got a name for it. Posttraumatic Stress Disorder. That's
a long name. Probably just call it PTSD.*
    *Wonder if things will get any better now. Hope he stays in
treatment – that would be really great. At least he'll be out of my hair
for a couple weeks. Gee, it's nice having him gone for a while. Think
I'll just relax.*
    This PTSD thing sounds really big. Tough times ahead, I bet.

    Me (a little relieved)

TROUBLE BREWING

Sarah remembers the day her life fell apart. It was one Friday morning in the winter of 1986. She and her husband had just seated themselves at the local restaurant to order breakfast. They ordered, sipped on coffee and talked about the weekend's plans.

Suddenly, Sarah's husband excused himself to take a trip to the men's room. Sarah sat in the booth and waited by drinking two more cups of coffee. Finally, the food arrived, got cold and turned rubbery. But still her husband didn't return. Twenty minutes had passed when she began to wonder and worry.

Sarah got up from the table, told the waitress that she would be right back, and made a quick tour of the restaurant. Not finding her husband, she walked outside to the parking lot. There he was, sitting in the car, staring forward.

"What in the hell are you doing?" Sarah couldn't believe he was ruining their Friday-morning breakfast ritual. "Get out of that car – your breakfast is ruined!"

Her husband only turned, looked at her blankly and said, "I don't know what happened, but this 'funny feeling' came over me. I just couldn't sit in that restaurant any longer. I had to run!"

From that winter morning of 1986, Sarah's life became a constant flurry of unexplainable events and traumas revolving around her husband's "funny feelings." There were the emergency room visits, the hospitalizations, the new medications, the crazy behavior ... the list goes on. For her part, Sarah was dazed. She remembers those years as foggy. No clue as to what was happening. No clue as to what the future would hold. No answers, no friends, no help.

Cindy also remembers the exact time when her combat vet husband just seemed to "crash." It was in November of 1986. The two of them had just transferred from another state to follow her career path. While the move made Cindy feel very successful, it made her husband, on the other hand, feel very unsuccessful. Unable to find a construction job like the one he left behind, he eventually settled on part-time work.

The months following the transfer were a free fall. As Cindy settled into her new job and the couple's new home, her husband became angrier and more difficult to live with. His drinking increased. He frequently burst with anger. Most often he just withdrew. "I thought he was going nuts, crazy," Cindy says. She blamed her husband's behavior on his lack of a job and all the guilt that goes along with it.

Cindy's marriage continued to free fall, and her husband's behavior continued to worsen. In 1993, Cindy knew she had to do something to save herself, her husband and their relationship. She just wasn't sure what that something was.

Mabel also remembers the turning point in her life. She remembers the day she was supposed to pick up her husband, Dick, after his discharge from the service. She recalled earlier memories of her husband – "happy, busy, into everything, very active, worked day and night, loved his children."

What Mabel didn't know was the extent of Dick's nervous condition, picked up during the war and the reason for his discharge. Mabel didn't know the details of that day in the South Pacific, when the Kamikaze pilot hit the deck of the ship, dropping a bomb to the second deck. She had no way of feeling Dick's helplessness; though on sick bay, he had managed to crawl to the deck just in time to watch the entire ordeal. What he remembers most vividly is the Japanese pilot, still alive, being pulled from his plane, stripped of the jewels that lined the sash around his waste and being thrown into the ocean.

Mabel realized something was very wrong the moment of her reunion with Dick:

I had to pick him up in Chicago, and of course, he's always ahead of schedule ... Anyway, he wasn't in the room he said I should be at, and I thought, "That's funny." So I put my luggage in the room and it was so nice outside, that I walked around a little bit. I walked around the corner, I think it was a coffee shop, probably a tavern, I don't remember. He was sitting on a stool by the bar. He was strumming on the table, and I thought, "What am I going to do?" But I just went in and said, "Hi, glad to see you," and he calmed down. He was nervous all the time, but not that bad.

I had to go and get him from Chicago because they (military) wouldn't trust him alone, he was that bad. And he'd come home and sit by the window. We lived upstairs; he'd watch people walking by.

Dick's nervous condition never improved and his memories of that fateful day in the South Pacific never faded.

Shirley remembers her son's tumultuous homecoming from Vietnam. Her happy-go-lucky son with the ready smile (whose charm "could get Alaska to install ice machines") came back from war very different. "He was really moody. Right away I said, 'Tom has a problem.' Everybody laughed at me. Nobody paid any attention to me in the family. They could not see, they all denied it. From the very beginning I could tell. If there's a part of you and it's walking around ... and something's wrong with it, you know, as a mother."

Tom's post-war years grew more tumultuous by the day, and Shirley grew more and more concerned. She could not understand her son's antics; he fought the law, got divorced, took drugs, no longer bathed or shaved. Tom's transformation was gradual, but complete.

As a mother, Shirley took the blame for Tom's changes. She says: "I just couldn't understand why he was so different. I was hurt, frustrated. The thing I kept doing, that went through my mind, was, 'What did I do wrong when I was raising him?'" Shirley accepted the blame, which her son was also happy to throw her way.

"I had no idea there were so many other people out there having the same problems," she shakes her head.

For both Nancy and Patty, alcoholism muddied-up the source of the problem in their marriages. Nancy knew her husband before the war. He didn't drink then, so his heavy drinking after the war convinced her that he had just become a drunk. She failed to connect his behavior with the war.

But Patty suspected something deeper at the heart of her husband's drinking. She had met Lonnie long after his stints in Vietnam. When he landed in an alcohol treatment program, Patty begged the hospital's psychiatric unit to examine Lonnie for something more. What that something more was, Patty had no idea. "I had no idea his behavior was related to Vietnam," she shrugs.

Though Cheryl also noticed the gradual coming-on of PTSD in her Vietnam vet husband, she can pinpoint the trigger that blew things up. It was during the Persian Gulf War, she recalls, when her husband's rage and violence came out to the point where he kicked her. She remembers knowing, "I've got a *big* problem on my hands."

Because the association was so clear, Cheryl knew the behavior was related to Vietnam. After watching extensive TV coverage of the Gulf War, her husband "would become disruptive, angry at how the Vietnam War was handled and angry at how he has been treated as a veteran." Though the source of the anger was clear, Cheryl felt no better equipped to handle it.

FINDING THE RIGHT ANSWERS: DIAGNOSIS AND TREATMENT

For many, maybe most, families living with PTSD, the journey to proper diagnosis and treatment is a zigzagged one.

As a fairly new disorder, recognized only since 1980 by the American Psychiatric Association, PTSD is not well-understood. There are many medical and health professionals, in fact, who know very little about the disorder. Other community professionals, such as law enforcement officers and clergy, are even more in the dark, so their ability to respond during crises or make appropriate referrals is very limited.

The community's confusion about PTSD carries over into the life of the vet and his family. Family members complain of feeling helpless in their continuous search for appropriate diagnosis and treatment. They also complain of facing negative forces and of butting heads against this doctor, that administrator or this-and-that rule.

Dr. Arthur Blank, Jr. has worked with veterans and their families since 1973 and was also an army psychiatrist in Vietnam. Dr. Blank confirms the negative foundation upon which current treatment for PTSD is based:[1]

I think in the case of Vietnam veterans, all of these problems which would occur to some degree with any war veteran, Vietnam veterans see these problems more compounded because professional help was not available or it was counter-productive or even sometimes professionals were hostile – intentionally or otherwise – towards veterans in the 1970's and a ways into the 1980's, depending on where one lived.

No one could get treatment for PTSD in this country who was a Vietnam veteran until beginning slowly, around 1980, with very few exceptions. People went all the way through the 1970's, which is a 10-year period, with no treatment.

Treatment became available specifically in 1980. But the resistance among professionals was so great, it took another five-six years for treatment to become widely available.

Today, there are inpatient and outpatient PTSD programs at VA Hospitals throughout the country, and many private providers offer treatment programs as well. Imagine the task facing those programs – dealing with the vet's pent-up anger from all those years! Imagine, too, the unleashing of those problems on the vet's unsuspecting family!

(Vets and their families should be aware that service-connected disability ratings are available for veterans who qualify. The ratings are given through the U.S. Department of Veterans Affairs (VA), and these ratings are tied in with financial compensation and other benefits due service-connected disabled vets. Specific benefits are dependent upon the percentage of disability granted. For information, call the U.S. Department of Veterans Affairs' nationwide toll-free number, 1-800-827-1000 [Telecommunication 1-800-829-4833] or, if the number has changed, check under the U.S. Government listings in your local phone directory. The number rings in each caller's state. More information about service-connected disability ratings appears in Chapter 14.)

Sarah's story is indicative of the challenges of finding appropriate answers and help. As her husband's emotional and physical states deteriorated, Sarah realized she was alone in her journey. Her husband was less and less able to handle his pain, and his behavior was out of control. Extended family members offered no help. In fact, they pretty much ignored the situation. Sarah recalls, "They were busy doing their own thing – raising kids, paying bills, starting careers. I do understand how disgusting Bill's behavior was to them, and how irritated they were at me for tolerating it. But I don't understand why they couldn't see my pain. I desperately could have used their help, any kind of help!"

Sarah tried everything. She took her husband to the local health clinic, where he was seen by a general practitioner. The general practitioner dispensed some anxiety medication (because he was currently dabbling in that area), but eventually decided the problem exceeded his ability to help. Sarah's husband was referred to a psychologist, who met with him a few times before also deciding the problems were out of his reach. The next stop was a psychiatrist, who further dispensed medication.

It took a major event, however, for the proper diagnosis to emerge. One night, Sarah's husband overdosed on a mixture of liquor and pills and landed in the local emergency room. There, the attending doctor recognized the signs of war trauma (because of his own service in Vietnam), and referred his patient to the VA Hospital. At the VA, Sarah's husband underwent a battery of tests, and was finally and officially diagnosed with Posttraumatic Stress Disorder.

Sarah was relieved and surprised. The official diagnosis brought with it financial compensation, which helped relieve her own stresses of being the family breadwinner.

"Relief" is indeed the word used over and over again by loved ones of vets who finally do get properly diagnosed and treated. Yeah! A label!

"I was always searching, trying to find out what was wrong with this guy," Nancy explains of her husband. When the diagnosis came, "All the searching was over ... a weight was lifted!" Though alcohol had masked the situation for years, her husband's bout with depression eventually resulted in a visit to the VA Hospital, where he discovered that PTSD was the source of his problems.

Shirley found relief, too, in the discovery that other families face the same coming-home traumas that she faced with her son. While proper diagnosis and help did not come from the professional community, but rather from meeting with other vets and their families, it came all the same. Like those who hear the diagnosis from a doctor, Shirley felt great relief. She felt especially relieved at knowing she did not cause her son's problems.

For some, the discovery of PTSD is not a relief. Upon their husbands' diagnoses, Patty and Mabel talk about how they knew instantly that their futures would be different. Patty, in particular, remembers knowing right away that Lonnie's PTSD foretold a completely different lifestyle. She promptly quit her hectic professional job and moved with her husband to a quiet farm in the country. Of their alternative lifestyle, Patty proclaims, "There is no alternative."

The diagnosis of PTSD also brought no relief to Cheryl. As a professional woman in contact with the public, she had seen other women like herself, other women abused by their husbands. Recognizing the signs of abuse, she knew there was only one way to survive. She promptly separated from her husband and insisted that he seek treatment for PTSD.

During the difficult separation, Cheryl battled a barrage of negative reactions, from herself and others. She found herself buying into the conservative thinking of her conservative background. After all, she was supposed to make everyone else happy, wasn't she? She was supposed to keep the family together, not break it up and make everyone miserable, right?

Cheryl got the cold shoulder from extended family members and work colleagues, who made her feel like she was doing something wrong. Both her thinking and that of others "was a real hindrance," she sighs. "It took me a long time to realize it wasn't my fault."

But toughest of all was swallowing her pride. As a competent professional woman, Cheryl was used to helping others, not needing help herself. Now she found herself "one of those kinds of people.."

And sometimes the correct diagnosis of PTSD is a long time coming. The path can be hilly and curvy, and fraught with bad advice and even misdiagnoses along the way.

Cindy shares the dark comedy of her journey. As her marriage deteriorated to the point of crumbling, Cindy went to see a counselor.

After a few visits, the counselor told her that she was a care-giver and needed to get out of the marriage. But Cindy chose to hang on, at least this time.

Then, one of her husband's buddies shared his assessment of the situation: He thought Don, her husband, was having a delayed reaction to his experiences in Vietnam. The buddy had seen that kind of thing before in other construction workers. The argument convinced Cindy, who went off on a quest to find out more about this "delayed reaction" thing.

She listened to tapes and visited with experts in the field of war trauma. After minimal research, Cindy decided the whole thing was a little too depressing. At this time, too, her husband's physical state had deteriorated to the point he could hardly walk. He had lost massive amounts of weight and feelings in his legs, and his overall appearance became sickly.

Don sought help at the local hospital, where doctors first conducted a quick interview and visual check. Before drawing the first drop of blood, they offered their assessment: Don was suffering from Aids. They informed him of their quick diagnosis, and he in turn informed his wife.

For Cindy, the time between the quick diagnosis and the proper diagnosis was a hellish nightmare. She obviously felt much better when the diagnosis was changed to PTSD. Don, on the other hand, was not quite as sure. "Gee, with Aids I know I would have lived at least seven years. With PTSD, I'm not quite so sure ..."

TREATMENT: SUCCESSES AND DISAPPOINTMENTS

Even upon successful diagnosis, many vets and their families continue to grapple with PTSD. The reasons for their struggles vary – sometimes the vet refuses help, doesn't finish his treatment program, participates in the wrong treatment program, etc. And sometimes families make mistakes, too; they refuse to participate in programs alongside their vet, fail to find the right program for their needs or set their expectations for treatment way too high. And sometimes everyone just gives up; they all quit treatment and/or the family breaks up.

Sometimes treatment fails because the vet, spouse or other family member has a problem independent of PTSD and does not find help for that problem. Or members of the family refuse to let go of the "I'm OK, you're the sick one" philosophy, thereby sabotaging the vet's progress.

A common complaint of families living with PTSD is the revolving-door nature of the disorder. Even after successful diagnosis, they say, the cycle goes on: The vet feels crummy, goes into the hospital, comes home. The vet feels crummy, goes into the hospital, comes home. The vet feels crummy, goes into the hospital, comes home ... and on, and on, and on. Families often see little change with the revolving-door syndrome. Though they know the source of their pain, their lives continue to be disrupted.

Along with the revolving-door syndrome, families complain of their vets' institutional thinking – e.g., after having been hospitalized so often, their vets begin to think and talk as if hospital life is normal life. "I hate when my husband gets excited about being in the hospital during Christmas," one wife explains. She describes her husband's institutional thinking:

He's excited because the Auxiliary ladies hand out Christmas gifts for the guys to give to their wives and children. Imagine that. He can't wait to get us those free presents. The ladies help him pick out each of the gifts, and then they even wrap them. Sometimes he tries to get more than what's due him. One year, he tried to get gifts for our dogs, pretending they were our children. It's amazing how excited he is to have me open them. He seems so proud, like he went to the store and bought them or something.

Spouses and families also complain of the "letting down" of treatment that either does not work (or the vet does not make it work), or it does not provide appropriate follow-through and after-care. Many also admit to expecting too much from treatment, expecting it to cause nothing short of miracles.

When Nancy's husband entered a treatment program, she rejoiced. "I felt, here's the answer," she says. As her husband passed through the program, however, she noticed he was in a lot of turmoil. He missed parts of the session, and ended up dropping out. Eventually, he repeated the program and finished.

Through it all, Nancy held steadfast. "I still had really high hopes of seeing change," she reports. When the change didn't happen, she herself went through major depression. She ended up seeing a psychiatrist and going on medication. To this day, Nancy and her husband still battle the demons of PTSD.

Barbara's story is also fraught with turmoil. When her husband joined a PTSD program, she, too, rejoiced. When her husband came out of the program seemingly unchanged, she despaired. Eventually, the marriage broke up. Barbara describes her initial elation upon joining a PTSD support program at the same time her husband joined up:

I remember going into one of the rooms and just standing by the wall and just crying. I couldn't stop crying. I don't know why ... I really wanted it to be something that was going to work. This was my savior – coming out here was the only thing that was going to save us.

Barbara blames the marriage breakup on her husband's emotional distancing and violence, directed mainly at her son from a previous marriage. Today, she regrets not leaving sooner.

Despite Don's proper diagnosis of PTSD and Cindy's steadfastness through very rough times, their marriage did not survive, either. Cindy tired of Don's "no-hope syndrome," even during therapy, and decided the emotional toll was just too much. After years of trying, the couple split.

Sarah describes the stress and let-down of being in a community that doesn't understand the diagnosis of PTSD. Though her husband has his diagnosis – it's official and in the records – he frequently faces an ignorant medical community.

Sarah recalls the time when her husband became violent. She called the police, who called the paramedics, who arrived and stayed at their home for hours before deciding "what to do with Mr. Anderson." Her husband was eventually transported by ambulance to the nearest private hospital (he was determined to be too dangerous for his wife to transport him). After a brief visit with the doctor, Sarah's husband was discharged even before she could drive herself to meet him. Once again, he was in her care because the doctor and hospital staff didn't know anything about Posttraumatic Stress Disorder, let alone how to treat it! Several hours after her initial plea for help, Sarah drove herself and her husband home. Hungry after the ordeal, the two stopped for a burger and fries on the way. "Talk about a weird night," she says, shaking her head.

On another occasion, Sarah's husband visited his local clinic for stomach pain. The nurse, who read his records and saw the word PTSD, turned to him and remarked, "Oh, you're one of *those* guys." By the tone of her voice, Sarah's husband was sure that "one of those guys" was not good company to be in.

And during still another crisis, Sarah watched in horror as a local police officer taunted and threatened her husband. She says she could feel the officer's disgust at having to deal with her husband and his mumbo-jumbo about the war.

Cheryl's story is a happier one. Intense therapy has made her husband realize that his thinking is often irrational. Cheryl claims that this realization alone has opened up great possibilities in their marriage. Her husband is now open to discussing things and accepting the possibility that he can be wrong. "I feel we are a success story," Cheryl says. Today, the two continue to work on their problems, both as individuals and as a couple.

(*Author's note:* Chapter 14 presents additional stories about families coping with PTSD through treatment, and in other ways.)

CHAPTER THREE

ONE FOOT IN THE FOXHOLE ...
ONE FOOT IN THE PRESENT

PTSD AND THE CLASH WITH REALITY

Dear Journal,

Sometimes like to daydream. Like taking a trip without leaving! I close my eyes and think of him. He's different; he's young and laughing and having fun with his friends. Think they're playing cards. It's great to see him so happy.

Wonder if my daydream means anything. Like maybe it's before the war, before he did those terrible things. Must be. He's not carefree like that any more.

Feel a little better when I wake up. Sure, it's just a dream, and pretty soon he'll come charging through the door.

But just think, I can daydream any time I want. Doesn't cost a thing. He's so much happier in those dreams, and you know what? So am I.

Me

OUT OF TOUCH

Many vets with PTSD live in two worlds: The world of the past, and the world of the present. Sometimes the two worlds live side-by-side, sometimes they clash and sometimes one overtakes the other. Always, the demarcation is very fragile.

Spouses and significant others refer to the "10,000-mile stare," the blank look that betrays a world far away and long ago. They know when they look into their vets' eyes that the pain of the past stares right back at them.

"How do you expect me to react to your job?" one vet asks his wife as she talks about her workday. "You work in insurance," he tells her. "Let's get real – insurance work is not exactly life-threatening." The wife walks away, frustrated that she is unable to release the tensions of the day. She stops, and remembers her husband's stories of maiming and death in Vietnam. "I guess he's right," she says. "My office gossip hardly competes with war."

Maiming and death versus minor office gossip. The combat vet struggles between living in two worlds – the surrealistic world of war and the demanding world of today. Intensifying his internal struggle is the fact that those living around him really do not understand what he went through. Society just doesn't get it.

Spouses and other loved ones agree they are ignorant about the fine details of war. But, they complain, "How can we be expected to know? We get so tired of hearing him say, 'You couldn't possibly understand because you weren't there.'"

Bill summarizes the feelings of vets everywhere when he describes his homecoming from Vietnam. "My family didn't even bother to pick me up at the airport," he says, dryly. "I took a taxi home." He describes walking into his parents' house for the first time in nearly a year. "My dad was sleeping on the living room sofa, and my mom was cooking in the kitchen. I walked in, and they both just said, 'hi!' You know, I really believe my mom thought I was in Hawaii all this time." From the jungles of Vietnam to Mom's kitchen, thousands of vets received the same welcome-home reception – a simple "hi!"

Bill's mom is defensive about her behavior back then. She questions how she could have possibly known the hell her son had been through. Besides, she says, she'd been working all those years. And even though TV carried lots of news about the war, she never really stopped to think about it much.

For many vets, the strangeness of their homecoming foretold a stranger future, a balancing act between past and present. Today, they battle the opposing pressures of intrusive thoughts, brought on by reminders of war, and the tug of everyday responsibilities. For some, the balancing act is overwhelming, and they succumb to the bad memories altogether. As one combat vet finally admitted to his wife, after years of trying to shake the ghost of war, "I just can't live in *your* world."

Your world. The world of loved ones, also deeply affected by the vet's struggle between past and present. After living with that struggle for so many years, many begin to question their own reality: Psychotherapist Kathryn Berg says:[1]

*When one person in the family feels out of touch ... in trying to protect
him or herself, he or she tends to make everyone else unsure of what
his or her reality is as well.*

*The effect (of being out of touch) on family is that they then begin to
mistrust their own perceptions and in turn seek even more validation
for what is real. They become even more externally focused,
externally dependent, as opposed to feeling more confident and self-
assured and able to trust their own intuition and perceptions.*

Family members living with PTSD find themselves straddling the same
two worlds as the vet. They not only live in the present, but – because of their
association with the vet – live in the past with him as well. They share murky
visions about events that they were not a part of, and question why those
events have to be so invasive. Always, they dream of having a "normal" life,
one like everyone else.

THE FAMILY "PLATOON"

Spouses and other loved ones of combat veterans did not actually fight in
the jungles of Vietnam or on the shores of Normandy or in the sands of Iraq.
And yet they are asked to be a part of those worlds day after day. Combat vets
with PTSD frequently refer to their war experiences and often hang on to their
war paraphernalia, e.g., medals, unit patches and faded old phone numbers.
Some even erect war shrines in their homes; the shrines live alongside
computers and the other trinkets of today, showcasing the incongruity of life
in the past and life in the present.

Families often try to capture a piece of their vet's wartime memories by
adopting the psyche, lingo and even the dress of combat. They know what it
means to "secure the perimeter" for the night. They know all about "Charlie,"
the "VC" and the "LZ." They remember the good ol' days of the Andrew
Sisters and Eddie Canter in the canteen, and all about the white cliffs of
Dover. And they can just feel the dripping humidity of Southeast Asia; they,
too, see the steam on the airplane window as it lands in-country.

Twenty-year-old Shannon shakes her head when she describes the way
her father refers to their family as a *platoon* . "He compares everything to
Vietnam ... He always walks around and says, ... 'If you were in Vietnam with

me, this platoon would fall flat on its face.' I keep telling him this is not Vietnam, this is your family."

Shannon recalls growing up in the shadows of war. It was always present, she says. Her father couldn't go to her games at school because of the war. Her father couldn't stay sober because of the war. Her father couldn't stop beating up Mom because of the war.

Today, the family no longer does any "family stuff together," which Shannon says, is most painful of all. And now that Mom and Dad are officers in one of the major vets' organizations, there's even less time for family stuff. Home life is a constant round of phone calls and running off to meetings.

And those glorious holidays, once reserved for frolicking, no longer belong to the family, either. Especially hateful are the patriotic ones, with their parades, salutes and military crap.

Though she has experienced little of the outside world, Shannon is sure there's more out there for her than this.

For 70-year-old Shirley, living with PTSD has drawn her into a world far different than others her age. In contrast to the coffee klatches of her peers, Shirley's days are filled with the nightmares and sad memories of war. She cares for her son Tom, a Vietnam vet with PTSD, and his son. The three of them live in a run-down home in the country. There, Tom spends his days partially taking care of his child, but mostly remembering the war.

Shirley, on the other hand, has no time to waste. For she has meetings to go to and speeches to make. A veterans' activist since her son's tormented return, Shirley works on behalf of the rights and healing of veterans everywhere. She is absolutely devoted to her cause; some even call her feisty.

At home, Shirley surrounds herself with reminders of war. Pictures of her handsome son, before and after Vietnam, hang on every wall in the house. An entire room is saved for posters, framed letters and other mementos of her involvement in the building of a Vietnam memorial in her home state. She is proud to tell of her very special contribution; she tells of sitting atop a billboard on a very busy freeway, and refusing to come down until enough donations came in.

She also tells of organizing a welcome-home reception, three decades after the war, for Vietnam vets in her hometown. Knowing that the vets would march in a Fourth of July parade, she made up "welcome-home" banners and prepped the crowd beforehand to clap when the tattered platoon walked by. "These vets were in tears," she says. "They were crying that nobody had ever said welcome home, thank you."

But it is the POW/MIA situation that turns Shirley's complexion the color of her red hair. She keeps a constant vigil for breaking news about the remains of U.S. servicemen. And no topic makes her angrier. "I wear POW shirts constantly," she declares. "My sister and I once went to this special tourist place and she said, 'Let's get some shirts.' I said, 'no, as long as they're keeping our prisoners of war over there, I'm going to keep wearing POW shirts and I want the whole world to know about it.'" The only time Shirley removes her POW bracelets is to bathe or do dishes.

So important is Vietnam to her, in fact, that Shirley says if it ever goes away, it will be like cutting her hand off.

Ruth is also an elderly woman in her early seventies. She married her husband only a few years ago, right before his retirement. The two have a happy, compatible relationship and share an interest in community and senior affairs. Still, Ruth says she is surprised at how much her marriage and retirement are influenced by events of the past.

Ruth's husband is an elegant, soft-spoken man, easily brought to tears by his memories of World War II. Lately, he says, he has been haunted by his stint in the South Pacific. He struggles to keep the bad thoughts away and from becoming overly depressed.

Most curious for Ruth is the way her husband brings up war in the course of normal conversation. Not that he goes into detail about this battle or that one, she explains, but he tends to view modern events in terms of war. Hardest to deal with is her husband's anger over society's lack of interest. "Our grandchildren and even some of our children just don't seem interested that their father was in the service. They don't ask questions about anything." Ruth walks a tightrope between dealing with her family and appeasing her husband.

On a lighter note, Ruth credits her husband's service record with some of the minor aspects of their lifestyle. She's sure it's the reason for his obsession with being on time, traveling light and throwing things away. "I'd like to save things for a garage sale," she laughs, "but we've got to get rid of everything RIGHT NOW. If you haven't used something for three months, get rid of it!" She knows he picked these habits up in the service because family members say he was a real slob before joining up.

For Sarah, being the wife of a Vietnam combat vet has pushed her view of normalcy to the limits. "It's almost like living in virtual reality," she says. She tells the wild tale of coming home one day to find her husband talking intently on the phone. Curious as to what he was up to, she prodded him to reveal who he was talking with. He broke away from the phone long enough to tell her he was on the line with a helicopter company to "come pick him up and take him to his friend's house," one state removed. Unwavering, Sarah instructed her husband to hang up so they could discuss the situation. After talking about it for a while, her husband agreed to can the idea. Sarah chuckled; intellectually, she knew the whole thing was wild. Still, she couldn't help but wonder how her neighbors would have reacted to a helicopter in their street!

On yet another of the countless occasions when Sarah's reality clashed with the world, she didn't chuckle. It was in 1992, during the time of the hearings of the Senate Select Committee on POW/MIA Affairs. One morning, after hearing the findings of the committee, she burst into her office at work and shouted: "Did you hear the news? The Senate Select Committee has reported that prisoners of war probably were left in Southeast Asia!" She remembers spilling the words out breathlessly – to a room full of dumbfounded colleagues. Their silence reminded her that she lives in a very different reality. Ashamed, she walked quietly to her desk and went to work.

LIFE: THE UPHILL BATTLE

Families with one foot in the foxhole always struggle. Life is tough with PTSD. It's difficult enough to face the crises of today, let alone those of yesterday.

There's the battle with time, the conflict between military time and present-day time. Military time is the instant, we-got-to-go-or-we'll-get-blown-to-bits time, the one that vets can't seem to shake, even after all these years. Present-day time is the slower time of civilian life. It's the time that says, "It's OK to lie in bed for a while. There's no drill sergeant waking you up." It's also the time that says it's OK to be one minute late for a meeting; you won't step on a land mine. For families, the effect of the conflict between military and civilian time is usually just annoying. They spend their lives dodging the vet's orders to "hurry up or we'll be late ..."

But the battle with time has a darker dimension. For families coping with the pressures of present-day life, the vet's constant reference to the past is jarring. While she's trying to write out the bills, he's rambling about "that goddamn war protester." While she's trying to line up child care for the kids, he's talking about so-and-so, one of his war buddies of 30 years ago. While she's trying to have dinner after working a 13-hour shift, he's complaining about being ignored. It's a tug of war trying to support the vet with PTSD and stay afloat at the same time.

Another by-product of the tug between past and present is the vet's legendary inability to handle everyday responsibilities. How can he possibly add one more job to the huge burden of just surviving? "My only reality," explains one vet, "is to make it through the day. Anything else is extra."

This focus on survival results in the vet's preoccupation with himself and his own needs. What this means for family members, of course, is even more responsibility. After all, someone has to fill in the slack. Someone has to get the work done. Someone has to be the anchor. Parenting alone, making decisions alone, working around-the-clock, taking on nontraditional roles – this is what happens to spouses and other loved ones living with PTSD. Fatigue, resentment and disappointment are common.

"I would rather do 24 hours of hard labor than put up with this mental stress," complains Nancy, wife of a combat veteran. Among her many stresses is trying to repair and maintain the home. Though she hires outside help for repairs, the house is still not kept up. "Who gives a shit?" she asks. "No one comes over anyway."

Nancy's greatest fear is dying first. "If I die before my husband," she laments, "I'm sure no one will make my funeral arrangements."

And then there's Cheryl, whose full-time professional job in education is far more demanding than her husband's blue-collar job. In spite of her longer days, she handles most of the parenting and housekeeping chores as well. She nearly broke down when her husband handed her one more job – paying the bills. "I didn't think I could handle one more thing," she says. "And finances are not my aptitude at all."

Barbara, the former wife of a combat vet, describes the time when she had to leave her husband in charge of the kids for a week. As she lay in her hospital bed recovering from surgery, she kept getting calls from home. "My kids cried that there was no food in the house. My husband did give them something to eat," she says, "but it wasn't like he was taking care of them." Barbara remembers the horror of trying to get better while worrying about her children.

For Tracy, life is a never-ending uphill battle. All week, she and her Vietnam vet husband make plans to accomplish this or that during the weekend. Alas, the weekend arrives and what does he do? "He gets up on Sunday morning and tries to find out what time the first sporting event starts on TV." When Tracy reminds her husband of their plans, he gets defensive. "Don't worry about it, I'll take care of it, etc., etc."

But he never does take care of it. Eventually, Tracy jumps in. She is resigned to the inevitable:

I work full-time, I clean the house, I do the laundry, I do the grocery shopping, I do 85 percent of his work for (one of the veterans' organizations, for which he is president). Then I try to go have a cup of coffee and piece of pie with my mother, and I say, "Oh, Mom, I'm so tired. Can we do this in a couple of days?" I resent that.

Many families living with PTSD have managed to cope successfully with life's overload. Some of their coping skills are presented in chapter 14.

SOMEWHERE OVER THE RAINBOW

On the collision course between past and present, yet another problem arises for families living with PTSD: The vet's escapism to a more comfortable world.

The escapism takes many shapes. Often, it's a physical retreat, involving the move to a different locale. Patty, for example, has followed her Vietnam vet husband around the country for years. The two have lived in a small house, then on a small farm and finally in a mobile home. Their moves have taken them cross-country, all in the span of a couple years. With each move, Patty loses a few more personal possessions, but claims little emotional toll. "Luckily, I have a little gypsy blood in me," she laughs. Patty lives with the constant awareness that their next move may be days away; once again, she will follow her husband's quest for peace.

For Sarah, the physical retreat takes place only part of the year. She and her husband Bill inherited his family cabin. From April through October, Sarah feels the constant tug between working in Minneapolis and driving on weekends to the cabin in northern Minnesota. Though time spent at the cabin is pleasurable, preparations for the trip are not. Sarah resents making all the plans – buying groceries, getting the car ready, doing the laundry, both before and after the weekend. "To me, the cabin is a real pain. What I'd enjoy doing is spending my weekends at home, resting up for the workweek ahead."

But still, she says, she has to weigh the calming effect of the cabin against her own fatigue. "When I sit in the window, and watch his silhouette on the dock, slowly dropping the line into the calm waters, I know he's at peace. How can I say no to coming up here?"

For many vets, travel is but a dream, a brief mental respite. One wife tells of accompanying her husband to his medical appointments at the VA Hospital. On several of these visits, she noticed a vet seated at the front desk, U.S. map spread before him. On each occasion, the man appeared to be outlining a trip; sometimes his yellow marking pen went in an easterly direction, and sometimes it went in a westerly direction. During one of the visits, the woman could no longer contain herself. She blurted out, "Boy, you must really travel a lot." To which the vet turned and remarked, "No, I never go anywhere. I just like planning trips."

Besides traveling around the country or spending time in the woods, many vets choose an entirely different kind of retreat. They choose to retreat emotionally, withdrawing their affections, attentions and interest from both family and the outside world. They drop from mainstream life, leaving loved ones confused, isolated and frustrated. (The devastating effects of this isolation on families are presented in more depth in the next chapter.)

Wives and loved ones complain bitterly about this emotional retreat. They tell of their vets talking more with the family dog than with them, or of just disappearing for days on end. One wife tells of her husband, who, when feeling very badly, withdraws to the family room to play his *Wizard of Oz* tape over and over again. For several hours, he is mesmerized. The only time he talks to his wife is to invite her to watch the part of the video where Dorothy flies over the rainbow. "Wouldn't it be great," he sighs, "if there really was a place like Oz?" Each time, the wife is saddened by these questions. But she is also angry at having to watch the video ONE MORE TIME! ("I'd like to break the frickin' thing behind his back," she fumes.) Another wife tells of her husband watching the same western video 100 times or more. "Does he think the ending will change or something?" she asks, both sarcastically and genuinely mystified.

Sometimes the vet searches for diversion through reckless behavior. He drives too fast, gets in fights, drinks too much – anything to run from life.

The recklessness is never good for the family, of course. Damaged property, spent energies and broken dreams are common by-products. And each reckless adventure costs money, creating short and long-term money woes. Families complain of having creditors after them; they are low on cash, low on reserves and low on credit.

When Bernie's husband returned from the Persian Gulf War, she was alarmed at his wild spending sprees. Her husband, Danny, had not been a soldier, but had an important civilian role that put him close to front lines. His

time in the Gulf resulted in several PTSD-type symptoms. Bernie describes
Danny's first few months at home:

> *Being in the war, you get more pay, you get financial stuff because
> you're there. And he came back and ... spent a bunch of money. He
> bought stuff for the family, but he also bought stuff for himself ... He
> wanted to buy stuff – big stuff – he was in a spendy mood when he
> came back.*

Sarah shares the concern over money. Her husband is always talking
about buying big stuff – motorcycles, grand homes, speedboats. She tires of
the talk, especially since those items are out of their financial reach. Once, her
worst nightmare materialized. She came home from work to find her husband
gone. Instantly, she knew something was wrong. All night, she paced, back
and forth, back and forth. Early the next morning, her husband appeared,
sheepish and guilty. After much hesitation, he announced that he had
withdrawn one of the couple's CD's, spending thousands at the gambling table.
Sarah cried; the money was to have gone towards a family car.

BUFFERING AND CLOSING THE GAP

Families straddling the worlds of yesterday and today speak of
"buffering" – buffering the vet from the outside world, and buffering the
outside world from the vet.

They take this role to heart. After all, the vet can no longer handle or
understand present-day life. They describe the difficulties of interpreting and
softening the effects of that world. They talk about telling half-truths to the vet
because the full truth is too harsh.

Maureen is the perfect buffer for her vet husband. Though the two are
divorced, she continues to pay his house payments, schedule his dentist
appointments and make other contacts with the outside world for him.

Cheryl shields her husband from the world by keeping him unaware of the
things going on in her own life. She avoids conversation that makes him feel
he has to take some kind of action, either verbally or actively. "By sharing
things, Bob always felt he had to do something about what I was saying,"
Cheryl explains. "Now I start every conversation with, 'I'm just going to tell
you something, and all I want you to do is listen.'" Cheryl's new tactic keeps

Bob from getting unnecessarily worked up, and herself from having to calm him down.

Making excuses for the vet is another way for families to buffer him from the world. They excuse his behavior to extended family members, employers, law enforcement, etc. After a while, of course, families tire of making excuses. It's just too darn hard explaining the unexplainable to people who aren't listening anyway.

Families have also made the unwanted discovery that by advocating on the vet's behalf, they often draw criticism to themselves. They are used to the barrage of unsympathetic comments: "I don't know why you stay with him" ... "Why don't you just shake him up?" ... "The war is just a big fat excuse for him" ...

For Sarah, being the buffer between her husband and the world has drawn strong sentiments from family members on both sides. Despite a lack of knowledge about PTSD, members openly share their views about it. Sarah's mom is especially vocal. She says, "You have to do everything for him. From a mom's point of view, it's hard to watch."

Sarah's brother is critical of the way in which she protects her husband, holding him at bay from other family members. "You won't let him fight his own battles," he accuses, "and you're overly sensitive to comments about him." He is especially angry that Sarah won't let him take her husband on fishing trips. But Sarah argues that her husband's depression, flashbacks and other PTSD problems make it difficult for him to participate in such activities.

The opinions of others, freely given, only put Sarah on the defense.

Patty is the spouse of a combat vet who finds that avoiding social contacts altogether makes it easier for her to avoid the critical onslaught. "I really don't care if anybody else believes me or not (about PTSD). I'm not looking for sympathy," she says.

Many spouses and loved ones see their buffering role as a two-way street. Not only do they buffer their vet from the world, but they also buffer the world from their vet. They often see their role in the extreme, as the protector of society. Because the vet with PTSD is often violent and attention-seeking, they take on the job of intervention. Dramatic examples include the petite wife who saves a barroom crowd from her gun-toting husband, and the wife who saves the neighborhood from a possible shoot-out between her husband and the SWAT team.

Whew! It's a big job saving the world. As the petite wife who saved the barroom crowd says of her husband, "You don't want to force the issue with him. I, for one, wouldn't want to call his bluff."

At times, children are the ones who intervene between the vet and the world. "Boys sometimes take on an advocacy role for their siblings and in some cases, are protector against Dad, are there for Mom," says Fred Gusman, Director of the National Center for Posttraumatic Stress Disorder, Clinical Laboratory and Education Division, in Menlo Park, California.[2] Their intervention again protects the vet, for he is spared the consequences of his actions.

To close the gap completely between life in the past and life in the present, families find they must do more than buffer or know the lingo of war. They find they must fully understand the vet's war experiences, fully immerse themselves in the look, feel and stench of war. They must be willing to give a little of their lives today to enjoy some happiness tomorrow. The key to it all, they believe, lies in the horror of the past.

But along the way, many stop to daydream a bit. They can't help but ask, "What if my vet hadn't gone to war? Would we have had children? Would he have been a great scientist or maybe a poet? Would he have been an excellent father, son or friend?" Though many experts advise against dwelling on pragmatic questions like these, still, family members can't help themselves. They can't help but wish they could have rescued their loved one from that foxhole, long ago and so very far away.

CHAPTER FOUR

MISSION: FOR ONE

PTSD AND ANTI-SOCIAL BEHAVIOR

Dear Journal,
Sometimes, I feel so lonely I could cry! He keeps shutting me out,
a little more each day. Pretty soon, we won't even talk to each other.
Wonder why he doesn't love me any more.
Maybe it's the nagging, or maybe it's my weight. Really have put
on a lot of weight lately. I'm sure it's my fault; everyone tells me it is.
The way things are going, there won't be an "us" much longer.
Something's got to happen. We aren't happy any more. In fact, we're
downright miserable.

(Sad) Me

AN ISLAND UNTO THEMSELVES

Kevin had the unique experience of growing up with two Vietnam combat vets. What he remembers most about both relationships is the complete lack of feeling.

Neither dad – his real one or his stepdad – bothered to know him very well. After divorcing Kevin's mom years ago, his real dad continued to live in the area but never tried to contact him. "My real dad and stepdad were even drinking buddies," Kevin says, incredulously.

Life with stepdad was no more intimate. Kevin, in fact, recalls the days and days on end that his stepdad would spend in the garage, "in his own little groove." Kevin learned early on not to intrude, or he would face the consequences of uncontrolled anger.

For a while, stepdad moved his family to the country to get away, he claimed, from drugs and the other bad influences of the city. Kevin recalls this time spent in the country as the weirdest time of his entire childhood. "My stepdad would leave at the crack of dawn and be gone all day. Meanwhile, me, my mom and my sister would be in the house, just reading. No friends. Nobody to talk to." Eventually, the family moved back to the city, but not before Kevin had, ironically, picked up a drug habit that plagued him for years.

As an adolescent, Kevin was determined to penetrate his stepdad's iciness, no matter what. "I started to ask him about the war," Kevin recalls, figuring that the conversation would bring them closer. The two even went to see the movie, *Full Metal Jacket*, together. What Kevin remembers about that experience was his stepdad on the edge of his seat, "white-knuckled during the entire show." Kevin's probing questions about war only resulted in a few terse responses, mostly about little things, never the big stuff.

Today as a young adult, Kevin continues to live in isolation. He has successfully battled his drug addiction but finds life on the outside too big and too challenging. He lives with his mom and sister and does not work or have friends. Instead, he prefers solitary days sleeping late, rolling his own cigarettes and reading science fiction books.

Kevin's isolation is typical among many families living with PTSD. Whether real or imagined, the isolation creates the same feelings of loneliness, the same feelings of being an island unto one's self.

There are many reasons for the isolation. The vet's own emotional withdrawal from life (referred to as "psychic numbing") can result in those around him doing exactly the same thing. Just as the vet builds a wall between him and the rest of the world, so, too, do his loved ones.

Sometimes the vet's behavior is out of the ordinary or even criminal, causing him and his family to withdraw socially (and others to withdraw from them as well). Or sometimes the vet, in an attempt to protect his family, draws them inward by "securing the perimeter," either emotionally or physically. And sometimes the retreat is entirely physical; the vet and his family opt to live a solitary life on the mountain or in the woods.

There are many levels of isolation, or "bunkering up," as the vets and experts alike describe it. The vet and his family can feel isolated from extended family, the neighborhood, the broader community and even from each other. Vets and their spouses sometimes distance themselves from one another so completely that expressions of love and intimacy are impossible.

Whether isolated physically or emotionally, or within the neighborhood or from a spouse, isolation makes those living with PTSD feel alone in a big, scary world.

LEFT OUT OF LIFE

Psychotherapist Kathryn Berg describes the loneliness and confusion of living with PTSD:[1]

When the veteran is giving off antisocial signals, the family may respond in kind as a way of not getting hurt. "Oh, you don't want to be with us – well, we don't want to be with you, either." Pushing away, rebelling, resisting, they match the very behavior the veteran has exhibited. Or, they may do the very opposite. The veteran is cold, appears uncaring, isolating, withdrawing, not interested in personal connection. The family may try even harder to attach to him

Like Kevin, Shannon grew up the child of a Vietnam combat vet. She, too, describes her childhood as very confusing and lonely. As if there were some kind of master plan to keep her out of life. Always on the outside, looking in.

During Shannon's school days, she remembers not ever having friends over. "I was always at somebody else's house," she says, at first not knowing why. Eventually, she figured out that Dad's behavior was the reason why she was always being packed off to go somewhere else. As a teen, Shannon knew that friends wouldn't come over because they were too terrified of her father.

Not having friends over was the easy part. Far harder for Shannon were her futile attempts to be close to her father. She tried everything to please him, taking up basketball, race car driving and other boyish activities. "My dad got his son," she says proudly. "I was a real tomboy."

Along the way, Shannon even managed to pick up many of her dad's pastimes – drugs, running around all hours of the night and getting into trouble. Though these habits did not exactly endear her to her father, they did make her an awful lot like him.

Despite becoming more like him, Shannon never enjoyed a closeness with her dad. Probably most hurtful of all, she recalls, was the time she had to give up her baby for adoption and her dad reacted unsympathetically. "I told him, 'I went through the same painful steps with the adoption as you did with Vietnam. It's not on the same scale, but it's as traumatic.'" Still, no tears from Dad.

Today, Shannon's love-hate feelings for her father continue, and the close relationship still eludes them both. On the surface, things have evened out; they converse and live under the same roof. But always there's that unsettling undercurrent. Shannon walks the line between trying to please her father and just blowing him off. "I'd like to be his friend," she says softly. "We get close, then it's gone again – just like that," she snaps her fingers. What she fears the most is that the two will end up in a relationship like that between her dad and his parents, who haven't spoken in 10 years. When Shannon's grandfather passed away recently, her dad didn't even go to the funeral.

On the outside looking in is also the life story of Debbie, whose father's battles with PTSD literally destroyed her teen-age years. A quiet, reflective young woman, Debbie went all the way through high school without friends at the house or young men calling at the door. She compensated for the pain by excelling in both scholastics and sports.

As Debbie's high school graduation drew closer, she panicked about the party. Her dad had promised a huge celebration, complete with a boat ride and dinner for many guests. But through it all she wondered, "How will Dad behave?" Rather than risk the embarrassment, she canceled her own graduation party and settled on a small family gathering. That afternoon, a few relatives showed up to wish her well – an understated affair for one who showed such promise.

THE "MYSTERY MAN"

Whenever there's an emergency or problem in the neighborhood, Nancy's sure her son will get blamed.

Why not? He's the misfit. He's the one most likely to fail. It's only right that fingers point to him. After all, he's the son of a Vietnam combat vet.

Nancy blames her isolation on her husband's "mystery man" image in the neighborhood. Sure, he hasn't been out of the house in a month, and no one's seen him tinker in the garden for years. So what? Is that any reason to take it out on her and their young son? "I feel like the neighbors are all thinking that my husband is so weird," she says. And she thinks they pretty much think the same of her.

And well they might. Consider the example of Lori, an attractive thirtyish young mother who lives with her husband and three young children next door to a Vietnam combat vet. Lori and her husband laugh when others refer to them as Wally and June Cleaver. But it fits. Their house is well-kept. Their young children are beautiful. Even their parakeet is darling.

Lori herself has no connection to war. The closest she has come is through her mom's two brothers, who fought in Vietnam. "I kinda remember them coming home," she says, her memory obviously hazy. And now she finds herself living next door to a combat vet with PTSD!

There have been many incidents with the neighbor. What Lori remembers most is the time the cop cars blocked all the streets in the neighborhood and one cop even followed her in her house as she was just coming home from work. He had a walkie-talkie in his hands, his gun was drawn and he meant business. "I couldn't believe this policeman was in my house, peeking out the window," she gasped. It was obvious he intended to use her house as a lookout point.

The drama intensified. After a few terse questions, Lori was told that her Vietnam vet neighbor was believed to have a gun. Her heart sank, the lump in her throat thickened and she began to worry for the safety of her children. "Is he going to start shooting?" she remembers wondering.

Eventually, the drama wore itself out, as the vet was seen walking out of his house and climbing into the ambulance. It was over.

To Lori, though, the ordeal was not over because she had questions that needed answering. She promptly called the vet's wife to find out a little bit more about what happens during those "attacks." She asked curiously, "What exactly does your husband do behind closed doors? Are my kids' playfulness going to set him off some day?" She expressed relief at the wife's explanations and reassurances, and the fact that indeed there were no guns in the house. The two women even laughed at Lori's reference to "attacks" because of its inference to a madman.

For her part, the vet's wife appreciated the kind inquiry and concern. But she is sure the incident only widened the gap between her and her neighbors. "I won't hold my breath for an invitation to tea," she says dryly.

The incident also pointed out a major dilemma for the neighborhood. How should the neighbors handle their children's questions? Should the children be told the truth about their neighbor? Or should their natural curiosity be brushed aside? Lori details her own fancy footwork in trying to explain to her preschool-aged daughter what had happened:

Susie did see the cop car last time. We were home that day. She said, "Mom, there's a policeman out here." I said to myself, "Oh, it must be Bill (the vet)" ... Susie's glued to the window. And shortly after that the ambulance came. I said, "You know, I think Bill's sick, I don't think he feels good." She's like, "What's wrong?" I said, "I just don't think he feels good, and the ambulance is going to come and take him to the hospital and help him." And then Bill walked out – he's walking! Susie asked, "How can he walk out?" And I said, "Well, maybe he just has a tummy ache." I didn't go into it ... I just blew the whole thing off.

Lori is sure that someday she won't be able to blow the whole thing off. She knows that someday she may have to go into detail about something she herself does not fully understand.

Though Lori assures the vet's wife that she does not have hard feelings about the incident, and all the others, she does say that she will consider moving if the vet becomes abusive, e.g., if he kicks the dogs or swears at the neighbors. But because the vet's general demeanor is nice, she feels that the incidents of trauma basically do not interfere with her own life.

Today, the two women maintain a polite, but distant relationship.

GETTING WHAT YOU DESERVE

Society's overall ignorance of PTSD contributes to the isolation of those living with and around it. "You have PTS – what?" is a common question posed to vets and their family members alike. One veteran, in fact, reports he has better response when he tells people he has PMS instead of PTSD. "It's just easier," he chuckles.

Julie is the sister-in-law of a Vietnam combat vet. Like much of the rest of the world, she doubts the credibility of PTSD and, quite frankly, is sick of hearing about it. A few years younger than the Vietnam-era generation, she claims not to be interested in the Vietnam War or any other war. "My husband and I are tied up in our own lives," she says.

Julie admits to being confused by her brother-in-law's transformation. "When he first came into the family, he was clean and fun, even arrogant. Man, he used to primp all the time. You'd always see him touching his hair, making sure it was just perfect. Now look at him. He wears the same clothes, doesn't take a bath, just doesn't give a rip." Julie's observations are real; her brother-in-law has a 100 percent service-connected disability rating for Posttraumatic Stress Disorder.

Along with being confused and disgusted, Julie also admits to being suspicious of her brother-in-law's intentions. "Who's he trying to kid?" she asks. "How can a person change that fast?" She further describes impatience with her own sister, the wife of the vet, who she feels dotes entirely too much on her husband.

Darla is also the sister-in-law of a Vietnam combat vet. Unlike so many others, however, Darla claims to understand PTSD because of her own experiences with trauma. Years ago, her beautiful young daughter was killed on a lonely country road by a drunk driver. Ironically, the family had just moved to escape the dangers of the city. The death scene was particularly gruesome; the little girl's body was mutilated, having been thrown several yards by the speeding car.

Darla says she understands the bloody nightmares that haunt her brother-in-law. "I worry about him, but I understand what he's going through," she says. "I try to be helpful." She feels her own experiences make her a trustworthy friend, one who can listen knowingly.

But Julie's armchair view of PTSD may be more common. Her skepticism is surpassed only by the disbelief of those who have even less or no contact with PTSD. Julie describes her own futile attempts to tell outsiders about her brother-in-law and his problems. Outsiders really react with disgust, she claims. "They think it's bizarre, even hilarious. They say, 'Oh, come on, now...'"

"Oh, come on, now" is a common reaction to PTSD. Society's general perceptions about trauma contribute to the distancing between trauma victims and the rest of the world. Dr. Aphrodite Matsakis talks about the idea of victimization and society's intense fear of trauma and those who have been traumatized:[2]

Victimization is something we think will never happen to us. But after it happens, we think it's always going to happen.
We have to feel like the world's relatively safe. If you come to me and you are victimized, I may be compassionate or I may be threatened by your victimization. If I'm threatened, I may need to put some distance

*between us. One way to distance myself from your pain is to say you
did something wrong. That's why you were victimized.
To confront a trauma survivor is to confront the possibility that it can
happen to you.*

To outsiders, PTSD is especially alarming because it places the cause on
external forces. That makes people feel very vulnerable.[3] If trauma does not
happen because of an internal defect, if it can strike haphazardly, then how do
I know I will be spared?

Victimization may occur at the most intimate level. Spouses and others
closest to the vet with PTSD can also distance themselves from both him and
his war experiences. Like society as a whole, they, too, can fear the fallout of
trauma.

A second perception is the just-world philosophy which says, "The world
is just and you get what you deserve and you deserve what you get."[4] This
translates into the idea that if you have PTSD or you live around PTSD, you
deserve it. Dr. Matsakis elaborates on the thinking behind just-world:

*If you try to be a good, careful, kind, just person, you'll be safe ... But
the just-world philosophy doesn't make sense when you hit a
malevolent force – criminal, earthquake, rape, war. It doesn't matter
how good or careful you are. That's what makes it traumatic.
A lot of times it gets down to a moral question. Vets feel that their
combat stress reactions are something they did or didn't do in
Vietnam.*

Both perceptions – victimization and just-world – help explain why so
many PTSD victims and their loved ones feel society's disgust and shunning.
To trauma survivors, both perceptions are ludicrous. Imagine a young man or
woman running off to war asking to be traumatized, or family members asking
for their lives to be ruined! Victims also find it hard to believe that people fear
that trauma is catching, that it may rub off. Entwined with these perceptions is
society's overall disgust with war, Vietnam in particular. An unpopular war
back then, it is a taboo subject today. Society is equally disgusted with the
Vietnam veteran, popularly displayed as whacked-out, gun-toting, holed-up
and drug-popping.

Though both the victimization and just-world philosophies are indeed erroneous, they do serve a larger purpose: Both actually help people to go on with their lives. "To function, I need to feel that I can be safe," explains Dr. Matsakis. It would be difficult to work if you knew you could be shot, or to walk outside your door if you knew you could be run over by a car. To be able to function, people need to think they can work and play in safety.

The perceptions of victims themselves, both those who have PTSD and those who live around it, further contribute to distancing between them and the rest of the world. Individuals and families who live with trauma, especially with the surrealism of war trauma, know they have experienced something others have not experienced. Armed with the feeling of being different coupled with society's negative reactions, the trauma victim often goes underground. After all, as Dr. Matsasis says, who wants to be diagnosed "with all sorts of horrible sounding things, with friends and family and everybody saying he's a-this-and-a-that?"[5]

One vet and his wife echo the feelings of many who live with PTSD when they describe themselves as "square pegs in a round-hole society." Another vet says, "I feel so inadequate next to my neighbors. I hate them; they're so normal." And yet another wife of a combat vet says she's been so successful at going underground that people around her know nothing of her traumas. She maintains a cool, collected exterior, and gives the impression of perfection. She marvels at the comment of one of her friends who said, "What would you know about problems? You don't have any."

And yet another vet describes his ability to "performance play," or behave the way he thinks society expects him to behave. He describes the tremendous pressures of trying to act normally in front of his mother, siblings, even the postman. The experiences always leave him sweating and fatigued.

While going underground may certainly be an option for trauma survivors, psychotherapist Kathryn Berg prefers a different reaction. She helps trauma victims incorporate their experiences into a new meaning in their lives. Sure, trauma makes people different from others, but it also adds a depth to their life journey.[6] As the wife of one combat vet says with pride: "Unlike the rest of my family, I know I can handle anything in life. I've been through it all, seen it all. Nothing could surprise me."

TABLE FOR ONE

What Cindy remembers most about her former marriage to a combat vet is being alone. The irony of it does not escape her. She's supposed to be part of a couple, but she's alone. She grocery shops alone, attends parties alone, raises their daughter alone. "With social functions," she says, "I just go and do what I have to. People wonder why my husband is never with me."

For Cindy, life is a table for one.

Experts refer to those closest to the vet with PTSD as having feelings of abandonment and loss of partnership. They grieve – grieve for the warmth of a companion, and grieve for the commitments made on their wedding day. Those who live with PTSD long enough become wise to the harsh realities; the warmth and companionship are gone, probably forever. How can their husbands possibly fit in being confidant and friend, when they're working so hard at surviving? It's like being a widow, but worse. If your partner dies, you mourn and carry on. With PTSD, your partner is dead, spiritually and emotionally. But you can't mourn and bring closure. You have to carry on, and the problem never goes away.

For Nancy, that "table for one" is – literally – just that. She tells of trying to hang on to some of the same friends she and her husband enjoyed prior to his being diagnosed with PTSD. Occasionally, she ventures out alone to join the old group in a game or two of cards. "Sometimes I feel I should hire an escort," she laughs.

Barbara describes married life with her former husband as "living with a corpse." Now divorced, she remembers him as a fairly competent person. He worked hard and paid the bills, "but that's where things ended." He was like a statue, with no emotions, just nothing there. "The only time you would ever see him get excited about anything was when he was talking about 'Nam."

For Ruth, the loneliness is a little more erratic. It comes during the times when her husband, a World War II vet, withdraws to reflect on his horrific experiences on Iwo Jima and Okinawa. "He's a private person, and kind of buries things. Like 'don't talk about it and it will go away,'" she laments. Ruth's angry during those times of deep reflection because they make her feel very shut off.

One of the major features of Sarah's marriage is the total lack of intimacy. "We don't have sex any more," she shrugs. "I guess there's lots of reasons – I'm too tired from everything, and quite frankly he doesn't appeal to me much any more." Besides, it's tough, she claims, taking care of her husband's PTSD needs one minute and his sexual desires the next. "He's not my Tarzan, and I'm not his Jane any more. Now, it's more like he's my son, and I'm his mom."

Dr. Matsakis describes problems like Sarah's as the tug between the "responsible adult" role and the "playful child" role. It is very difficult, she explains, for "any ... overcommitted person, male or female, to turn off the 'responsible adult' mentality and become the 'playful child' in bed, or elsewhere" (*Vietnam Wives*, Woodbine House, 1988).[7] Sarah is the first to admit she doesn't laugh any more; the lighthearted moments she used to share with her husband have been replaced by an intensity and seriousness. She can't remember the last time she dropped everything to just sit and chat.

For Cindy, intimacy with her husband was at first satisfying. But over the years, his bedroom manners, like his overall personality, changed dramatically. He showed her no kindness during the day, but expected her to hop in the sack ON COMMAND! "I felt he was using my body," she says. The intimacy, though founded in marriage, made her feel no better than a prostitute. ("Feeling like a prostitute" is commonly expressed by the wives and girlfriends of vets with PTSD. They complain of their vets' lack of respect for women, and their frequent references to whores in war.)

Situations like Cindy's can be more complex for the experts to explain (studies regarding PTSD and sexuality are sparse). For many vets who appear to be cold and uncaring, however, the opposite is true: They actually love their partners, according to Dr. Stephen Barton:[8]

A lot of (vets with PTSD) have a hard time being touched or being near other people. And so that can interfere with the romantic bonding in a relationship. A person might be relating, but be emotionally cold in the process. They might be having sex or might be touching, but they themselves are quite distant. And that's picked up as lack of caring, when actually philosophically or intellectually, the way they (vets) are thinking, is that they are very affectionate. But their emotions have been damaged.

Brooke tells a similar story of her daughter's relationship with a Vietnam combat vet. The couple is extremely compatible and even considering marriage. Brooke has reservations, however, because her daughter's boyfriend wants them to marry, but live in separate houses!

Sometimes the vet is so blatantly inconsiderate, or seemingly inconsiderate, that he drives everyone away from him, including his loved ones. Though this may not be his intention, his actions and words speak of a self-centeredness unacceptable to others.

Barbara remembers the time her husband insisted she crawl out of her sick bed to make him lunch. Cheryl shudders at the memory of coming home from the hospital to find a sink full of dishes. She also remembers her husband yelling, "Get out the body bag!" when their son became very ill. Sarah still can't believe her husband's response when she scolded him for forgetting their wedding anniversary. "I don't know why you're mad," he said perplexed. "I remembered it in my head." And during her unhappy marriage, Cindy recalls working 60-hour workweeks and still rubbing her husband's back all night.

When Maureen told her husband that she had just been diagnosed with ovarian cancer, he answered coldly, "You're lucky. At least they have a name for it."

Sometimes jealously is the wedge between a vet with PTSD and his family. Unable to maintain relationships himself, the vet is jealous of the relationships his spouse, children and others are able to have. He may become belligerent towards those involved in the relationships. Or he may become attention-seeking, driving those around him yet further away.

Cheryl tells of her jealous husband, who was angry when she was about to make chocolate chip cookies for a sick neighbor. He insisted she make a double batch so he could keep one for himself. And Sarah lives with the constant pressure of her husband yelling: "Get off the phone. I suppose you're talking about me to your sister." Sarah obliges, even though her husband talks for hours on the phone himself.

And Nancy deals with her husband's minute-by-minute demands and jealousy over her efforts to start a new business. "He says, 'Nobody ever talks to me.' He sits in that little room all day and wants me in there, too, just to sit and talk. But I have to look forward to making a living," she explains. Nancy tells of bills piling up and creditors constantly at the door.

Often, family members intensify the distance between them and the vet by actually reaching out to persons outside the home – to extended family, friends, co-workers, clergy, anyone with an open heart. Unable to get the emotional support they need at home, they reach out to find it elsewhere. The wife of one combat vet says she gets her needed strokes from her boss, who praises her for being an excellent employee.

And still others who have lived with and battled PTSD are the ones who do the distancing. They are the ones who put space between them and the rest of the world. Following her divorce from a Vietnam vet, one woman describes herself as "scared of everybody." She tells of meeting a man in college, and striking up a conversation with him. When the two started their conversation, they were standing next to each other. By the time they ended, the woman had moved an entire table length away. What the woman didn't know was that the man was actually conducting a research study on personal space. She was shocked to find out how much space she put between herself and everyone else. PTSD had robbed her of the joys of being around people.

CONTEMPT FOR TRADITION AND AUTHORITY

PTSD families are used to Christmas without the tree, Thanksgivings without the turkey and birthdays without the gifts. "These days just come and go," one wife explains of her husband's work parties, which he never tells her about. Foregoing the usual celebrations and traditions of life is often the fate of families living with PTSD.

For vets, holidays can be very painful. Too often, they are wrapped around some horrible memory of war or, at the very least, of being away from home. It's not easy to celebrate when the enemy is closing in, or when your buddy just got shot in the gut.

One wife tells of being so consumed by her husband's sad story about Christmas that she has had a hard time enjoying the holiday ever since. Each year, she recalls his melancholy tale: "It was Christmas, right before I went to 'Nam. I went to church with all my cousins. I had my dress uniform on, with my gloves and hat. I thought to myself, 'I look real nice.' But then it was all for nothing, all for nothing." How sad and utterly wasteful, the wife muses, of her young man's future.

Many vets avoid not only holidays, but personal and family milestones as well. Family photo albums record the vet's absence; he is missing from the family birthday party, the wedding and the baptism. How lonely his family members look without him! One woman details the memory of her husband's birthday spent at the hospital: "His mom and I went to see him there. We brought him a few crummy gifts – he doesn't like a lot of fuss. He sat there on the bed, opening them. His mom leaned down and kissed him, 'Happy birthday, son.' I thought my heart would break. I prayed to God that we never spend another birthday like that."

For families, loss of tradition can bring forth many feelings. Sadness and anger are common, but so are feelings of freedom. Forgoing the usual hassles can allow the vet and his family the opportunity to create their own special traditions. They can enjoy a slower pace at the holidays instead of the usual frantic frenzy. But loss of tradition in the household can also cause frustration for the spouse and others expected to carry on, with or without the vet. For them, Christmas and other major holidays are major pains in the butt.

Sarah shares the exhaustion of trying to minimize the hoopla of the holidays (which her combat vet husband hates) while pleasing everyone else around her. She remembers one Christmas Eve especially well:

Bill was in the VA Hospital, which he often is during this time of year. I packed up the car to begin my deliveries. By the time I was ready, the entire trunk and back seat were filled with packages. Just like Santa Claus, I went from house to house delivering the gifts I was supposed to, being the perfect aunt and the perfect godmother and the perfect daughter-in-law. I had a miserable time doing all this crap by myself. When I finally got home, I could hardly drag myself into bed. I swear that next year I'm not going anywhere. I don't care who gets mad!

The very next year and every year to follow, Sarah has done the very same thing. Like other families living with PTSD, she struggles with the tug between wanting to be social and needing to pull in to meet the realities of her own life.

Contempt for the traditional rules of society can take many forms besides contempt for holidays. Since war, many vets – particularly Vietnam vets – have had an outright contempt for authority. Much of this contempt stems from "the Vietnam experience, where authority was extraordinarily untrustworthy," explains Dr. Arthur Blank, Jr.[9] Vets exhibit this contempt in many ways, ranging from simple ranting about the government to actually engaging in criminal behavior.

Targeting authority figures, even present-day authority figures, is one manifestation of this contempt. Disgust at the police officer, the head football coach, the school principal – anyone who is "in charge" can be a target.

Some vets, especially those who went into combat at a young age, they learned to suspend their normal morals and inhibitions about how to act in society. When they return, "not a whole lot is done to re-inoculate them with their old values and to re-frame things to get them back to a more socialized approach to things. When they return to the community their conscience does not operate as strongly as it did before because they've learned to break rules, the normal rules that govern our society," says Dr. Stephen Barton.[10] In addition, war may have eroded the young person's idealism and spirituality. He may also have a hard time changing his physiological response to act impulsively. The skills that served him well in war do not serve him well at home.

For the spouse and those around him, the vet's behavior may be peculiar, scary and embarrassing. They may also be surprised at the vet's lack of regret for his actions. "I just don't understand how he thinks any more," says one wife in frustration. "He doesn't seem to care how he hurts people." Often when the vet is regretful, what is most shocking to others is that he regrets only the consequences to himself, not the hurt he has inflicted on those around him.

The spouse of one Vietnam combat vet rues her husband's terrible prejudice against Asians:

I hate when we come across an Oriental person. I just hold my breath, hoping my husband won't call him a 'gook.' I remember one Halloween, when a couple of Vietnamese children came to the door. "Oh, no!" I gulped. "I hope he doesn't harass those poor little kids!" Luckily, he didn't.

I don't know what the word 'gook' means, but I do know my husband doesn't mean it as a compliment. Do you know he even called his doctor that once? I think it was to his face. That poor, kind man did not deserve my husband's assault.

The employer of a nonprofit agency in the Midwest tells of his special problems with employing a Vietnam combat vet. Because of the vet's contempt for close supervision and his desire to work alone, he was placed in a very solitary work setting. The arrangements worked to everyone's satisfaction – that is, until the vet decided not to report to work for several weeks. Not only did he not report, but he did not inform anyone, including his boss, of his whereabouts. While sympathetic to the vet's plight and also fairly knowledgeable about the peculiarities of PTSD, the employer was faced with the difficult decision of what to do. The vet was let go, probably blocking any future employment possibilities for other vets.

Law enforcement annals are full of stories of vets who act out in extreme ways against authority figures and society at-large. How should society respond to the vet who calls his local police station and threatens to blow it up? And how should society respond to the same vet, who apologizes by delivering a bunch of ice cream bars to the police station? Or how about the same person telling his wife he loves her, but threatens to cut her head off and put it on a stick if she doesn't love him back? Astoundingly, the man is angry when his wife calls the police for help. "The only number my family knows is 9-1-1," he says angrily.

Perhaps the most innocuous symbol of the vet's contempt for tradition is his poor grooming. Though certainly not true of all vets, many do have problems with personal hygiene, bringing great concern and embarrassment to those around them. For days or even weeks, they may not comb their hair, change clothes or take a bath. Certainly, hygiene is one reason why many spouses avoid intimacy.

Cheryl laughs when she remembers meeting her future husband not long after his return from Vietnam. "For the first three dates, he had the same clothes on. The same blue shirt and the same flared jeans." Cheryl knew her date had money to buy things, but just didn't seem to care that his wardrobe was rather limited.

For Shirley, the contrast between her nice, clean son before the war and her dirty, slobby son after the war is more than she can bear. She tries hard to joke about her son's appearance. But his good looks before the war are hard to miss; early pictures of him hang all over the house.

Some family members deal with PTSD by breaking out of the traditional mold themselves. Some mimic the sloppy dress of their vets and take up his other antisocial habits. Still others take up alternative lifestyles or philosophies that allow them to come to grips with trauma, their husbands' and their own.

When Barbara left her Vietnam vet husband, he had been so controlling that she decided to look and act as she wished. She changed her brown hair with its traditional haircut to a punkish look. She pierced her nose and eyebrow and began wearing young clothes.

But Barbara broke from tradition in ways deeper than altering her appearance. She dove into theater and art, which, she says, allowed her to express the depth of her anger – anger towards her husband, the government, the war. Today, she creates pieces in clay and teaches art classes at the local art center. Of the new Barbara she says, "I'm probably happier now than I've ever been."

Society, tradition, acceptance, friends, being one of the gang – loved ones of vets grapple with these concepts. On the one hand, they want to be part of mainstream life. On the other hand, they know all too well the private hell of PTSD.

CHAPTER FIVE

THE HANOI CONNECTION:
VETS, SPOUSES AND WAR BUDDIES

PTSD AND THE QUEST FOR COMFORT

Dear Journal,

He stayed up all night with his buddy again, the one from his unit. Made me mad that he wouldn't come to bed. Wish that old friend of his would just go away. Now, that's all he talks about and wants to be with.

Feel like a stranger in my own house. Wish that buddy would walk out the door and never come back again. We need time to be alone together, like we were at first. Now there's three of us in the marriage. Only I'm the one usually left out.

(Lonely) Me

LOVE-HATE FEELINGS

The war "buddy," "brother, "pal" – each word means the same thing. Each word symbolizes something deeply special between two people who share an uncommon experience.

But the words also bring a flood of emotions from the spouse and others closest to the vet. They bring feelings of love and warmth and appreciation – and they bring feelings of disgust, irritation and jealousy.

It's understandable that the war buddy should bring about such emotions. After all, he's always there, always in the family picture. Isn't he the one who helps with those dreaded panic attacks and flashbacks? Isn't he the first to shovel snow and mow the lawn for the family whose vet can't? And doesn't he help interpret the vet's feelings because those around him are too close to hear?

But the war buddy also comes between the vet and his family. He takes the vet away for hours and days on end to talk about the war. He enjoys an intimacy with the vet that even those closest to him do not. And he, by his very presence, reminds the family of something they are trying to forget.

Those love-hate feelings. The war buddy brings out only the strongest of emotions.

SECOND IN LINE

Before divorcing her Vietnam vet husband, Cindy describes life at home as an army camp. The transformation had been gradual, starting with her husband's phone calls to vet friends and ending with a constant round of overnight war buddies.

Cindy remembers how it first started. She remembers the gripping fear in her husband's voice when she called him from work. The panting, quivering, long periods of silence. She knew these phone calls helped her husband get through the day, particularly during those tough hours when he felt most vulnerable to the memories of Vietnam.

"Set-up time" was especially tough. It's that time right before dusk, late in the afternoon when vets remember having to secure the perimeter for the night. It's also the time of greatest terror, ushering in surprise enemy attacks and battles performed in the total darkness of the jungle.

Cindy remembers her husband's strong reaction when she told him she would not continue to call him from work. "He was furious," she says. "He just couldn't understand why, when he needed me the most, I couldn't be there for him." But Cindy stopped calling during set-up time. Her reason was simple: It would be during one of these phone calls, she says, when her husband would commit suicide. And she didn't want to be on the line when it happened.

That's when the real trouble started. That's when her husband started to reach out to his vet friends. Sure, he had had war buddies before. But they didn't seem quite as important as they did now.

At first, her husband reached out through the telephone. Several times a day, all day long, he called vet friends across the country. The long-distance phone bills continued to climb, until they averaged $800 a month. Cindy was horrified. But her husband refused to apologize. "That's a small price to pay," he quipped, "for keeping my sanity."

Soon, the phone calls were not enough. The fears, the nightmares, the memories – Cindy's husband needed more than a simple phone call to make him feel better. That's when he began inviting vet friends to his home, at first for brief visits. He and his friends would talk for hours, mostly about the war. Or sometimes they would discuss current events, but always in the context of weary eyes and battle-worn heads.

Eventually, the vet friends began spending the night. It seemed like the natural thing to do after an evening of beer-drinking and heavy discussion. Sometimes the night turned into a couple of days, and then a week. And sometimes it turned into a month or more. A couple of the really close buddies rotated moving in, so there was always an outsider at the house. Cindy found herself playing hostess to a constant round of guests.

What surprised Cindy the most was her own diminishing status in the household. More and more, she played second fiddle to the war pals. And imagine playing second fiddle to strangers! Though many of the guests did serve in the same unit as her husband, the First Cavalry, many in fact did not. The only thing they shared with him was their service in Vietnam. Cindy was never quite sure where her husband found all those guys to bring home. "He was always saying, 'This is another 'Nam friend, and I have to do anything I can to help him,' blah, blah, blah. But what about me?" The disgust and hurt are evident in her voice.

The more Cindy's husband opened up his house and checkbook to his buddies, the more used, disrespected and distant she felt. In fact, Cindy no longer felt like a wife. With no privacy and absolutely no personal life, Cindy began weighing her options.

In 1994, the couple divorced and went their separate ways. Today, each views the circumstances surrounding the breakup of their marriage differently. Cindy's husband blames her for being unwilling to help him fight his fears. "All I wanted was a simple phone call," he says. "I just don't understand why she couldn't call me. I felt betrayed." Cindy blames all those vet friends and her own feelings of displacement.

THE "HANOI CONNECTION"

Cheryl is a school administrator in a small Midwestern town. On the surface, she is calm and professional. She talks rationally and proudly of her husband's successful battles with PTSD and of her own personal and professional achievements.

But Cheryl's collected exterior cracks when she talks of her husband's closeness to a Vietnam vet he hardly knew. The story surprises her even to this day. It happened years ago, after the couple had been married for a while. One of Cheryl's friends visited her for the weekend and brought along her husband. While the two girlfriends enjoyed wonderful conversation about the past, the real magic of the weekend occurred between the two men.

Complete strangers until this meeting, the men instantly bonded. They discovered that their mutual service in Vietnam drew them together. They stayed up all night to talk and laugh and swap old war stories.

Cheryl was shocked. "He would never tell me about the war at all," she says sadly. "Wouldn't you think it would be more important for me to understand?" Years earlier, in fact, her husband had instructed her to throw everything away that reminded him of Vietnam. Secretly, Cheryl kept those items, hoping that someday their mysteries would be shared with her. But they never were.

After years of living with her Vietnam vet husband, Sarah, too, realized that she would never be her husband's complete soul mate. She recalls the time she posed a hypothetical question to him:

I asked him, "If you were having a severe panic attack, and you had just one quarter to call someone for help, who would you call – me or one of your buddies?" My husband replied quickly, "I would have to call one of my buddies. They are the only ones who can help me."

Sarah had guessed the answer beforehand, so she was not entirely surprised. What did surprise, however, were the responses her husband gave to a survey he completed while in the hospital. The purpose of the survey was to find out who her husband considers his friends and who he turns to for help.

Sarah was shocked to read the responses. To nearly every question, her husband indicated that he would turn first to his buddies. Other resources – psychiatrist, mother-in-law, brother – also scored high. Painfully, Sarah discovered that her husband does not view her as a confidante, either in work or play.

From the time of her husband's diagnosis of PTSD in 1989 to the present, Sarah has felt inadequate in dealing with it. She regrets not being able to comprehend her husband's pain. And she expresses feelings of displacement by her husband's war buddies, who somehow manage to connect with him better. She even admits to sabotaging her husband's close relationships with his buddies; she intercepts phone calls, turns his friends away at the door and makes constant excuses to get out of activities planned with other vets' families. She also questions the wisdom of buddies hanging out together. They do just a little too much drinking and a little too much carousing together, she claims. Who needs reinforcement of bad habits and bad memories?

Sarah has a name for her husband's bond with his war pals. She calls it the "Hanoi Connection." She wonders if the connection will last a lifetime. She questions whether she can break it.

ENIGMA OF THE BUDDY

The close, even mystical relationship between war buddies has been the subject of discourse for many years. Philosophers, artists, writers, historians and other great thinkers have paid tribute to this bond and tried to explain it through their works.

On the grandest scale are the war memorials, built by vets to honor their war-dead. Perhaps no other places on earth epitomize the life-death link between those who came home and those who did not. The Vietnam Veterans Memorial in Washington, D.C., is believed to have special powers of healing. Its harsh granite walls seem to reach out and talk to those who visit. Vets who touch the names of fallen comrades are said to touch their souls and spirits.

Shakespeare himself uses the pen to immortalize the bond among fighting men. In "The Life of Henry the Fifth," Act Four, Scene III, Lines 60-63, Shakespeare writes of the bond among men who are willing to die together. This willingness erases all class boundaries and makes men equal, at least while they face death together.

Hollywood does its part to portray the relationship among comrades in arms. From the World War I movie classic, *All Quiet on the Western Front,* to the slew of Vietnam-era films like *Platoon* and *Hamburger Hill*, the scene is played out over and over: The single soldier is pinned by enemy fire. His buddies brave sniper attack to drag him out of harm's way until the helicopter with the big red cross SWOOSHES down to rescue the injured soldier.

Even at its funniest, Hollywood paints a special picture of war pals. In the 1938 Laurel and Hardy film *Blockheads*, Hardy encounters his buddy sitting on a park bench, years after the First World War. Hardy is brokenhearted at the encounter, because it appears his pal has lost a leg (even though he's just sitting on it!). He carries his friend a great distance before discovering the truth. Though angered by the deception, Hardy invites Laurel home for dinner – unannounced. The predictable happens when the wife becomes enraged and throws both men out. Off they go together, happy to have found each other once more.

Off they go, hinting at the more lasting bond between war pals than between husband and wife.

THE DANCE WITH DEATH

Loved ones of vets find it hard to understand the mystical relationship between war buddies. They wonder how pals who haven't seen each other in years, like Laurel and Hardy, can just pick up where they left off.

But vets say it's easy to just pick up. For theirs is a bond of shared experience, of shared fate. The sense of being in the wrong place, at the wrong time together, brings them closer still. Only a few are destined to share the momentous events of the times.

Shared experience transcends to shared terror. "A 'Nammer?" one will ask the other, who nods knowingly. The union brings each a sense of peace.

The spouse, the child, the parent may never know what it's like to be in combat. They'll never know what it's like to kill someone. And they'll never know what it's like to share buddies like these. A hat commonly worn by veterans reads: "If you weren't there – shut up!"

For vets, the bond of shared experience means they have a hard time opening up to those who don't share the combat experience. "If you talk about war," explains one World War II veteran, "you only talk about it to another veteran. You don't choose to talk with others because I firmly believe there's no sense in talking about it because they can't really visualize what went on inside." *What went on inside* – inside the dance of death during war and inside the hearts and minds of vets since – is something only those who have lived it can understand. Dr. Stephen Borton explains:[1]

After being in combat, the wives and family of veterans are often perplexed why the patient with PTSD can relate to other combat veterans, but has great difficulty in relating to people at work or at home. The reason for this disparity in behavior arises from the nature of PTSD and its causes. Posttraumatic Stress Disorder has its origins in events, which to the individuals are outside the range of their normal life experience. For this reason, the PTSD patient feels that no one would be able to understand unless they had been through a similar experience.

Over and over again, vets tell of their horrific, almost out-of-body experiences that not only bind them together, but also make it difficult to communicate with non-veterans. Though the wars are different, the stories of bloodletting are the same.

John tells of serving in a "bastard" artillery unit. Once he and his small group of buddies were dropped, they never saw base camp again. For months, they fought side-by-side. Eventually, the mortality rate reached 95 percent in that small band of men.

Pete tells a chilling tale of hiding in the jungle for weeks, tied to his buddies on both sides with string. "We would tug at the string," he shudders, "when we wanted to make sure everyone was still alive."

But Bill shares perhaps the most compelling reason for camaraderie in the field. "Nobody wanted to die out there," he says. "We all had a pact with our buddies: GET MY BODY OUT!" He shakes at the thought of his body left rotting somewhere on some hellish foreign soil. To Bill, having buddies meant that his body would make it home.

For some vets, the shared experience takes them throughout their lifetime. They join servicemen's organizations to surround themselves with the safety net of war pals. Or they wear their unit shirts, bracelets, patches, pins and other reminders of this special unity with others. Dr. Stephen Borton continues:[2]

There is (another) reason why veterans of combat can relate to one another and that has to do with the frequent experience of death and the tremendous amount of grief that is associated with being in combat and seeing the rest of one's company shot down and being a survivor. A veteran experiences, by meeting with other combat veterans, a certain re-creation of the group that has been killed.

One servicemen's magazine describes a hereafter in which soldiers of all times and places meet and nod to one another, knowingly. In such a hereafter, the Roman Soldier, the Marine and the trooper from Rommel's Afrika Korps recognize one another, "all walking in the kingdom of God that they knew, or at least believed, was on their side" (*American   Legion*, September 1995).[3] Another servicemen's newsletter describes members who have died as being "transferred to the Post-everlasting."

And death, when it does come for vets who suffer, is yet another reason for old comrades to meet. The wife of one vet with PTSD describes the funeral of another:

> *Bill and I went to Andy's funeral the other day. It was quiet, not very many people showed up. But Andy's vet friends came. Each walked in, and embraced the other vets. None of them talked much, but they seemed to understand it all, this life and death thing. Like they've been there before. In fact, I hadn't seen Bill so calm in a long time. Just being around the other guys, even though it was a funeral. Now that I think about it, all the guys seemed at peace. Like the circle of pain is over now, at least for one of them.*

Spellbound by the mystical union she witnessed, the wife further pondered the simple elegance of the funeral. She noted the few terse lines of the obituary, and the overall lack of fanfare. "There was no mention at all of his having PTSD and cancer from Agent Orange," she said. "We all know the man died from being in Vietnam, yet there was no reference or blame at all. He just sort of quietly slipped away. It seems like we should have shot off cannons or something." Though extended family and life acquaintances stayed away, all of the man's vet friends were there. (The woman was further saddened to learn that one of the dead man's friends was also found dead only a few days later. Rumor is that he killed himself because he was unable to bear his buddy's death.)

It would be remiss to point out that for some vets, the common experience of war and death actually makes them avoid vet friends, much as it makes them avoid all social contacts. Or it causes them to have superficial relationships only. "Friends, after all, may leave (or die)" ("Road to Recovery, Posttraumatic Stress Disorder, the Hidden Victim," by Donald A. Bille, Ph.D., RN, *Journal of Psychosocial Nursing*).[4] The wife of one combat vet says her husband completely avoids vet friends, particularly on the telephone. She is unsure of the reason, except that "the phone is a bad news thing for him."

AT PEACE WITH THE HANOI CONNECTION

Coming to terms with the "Hanoi Connection" is not easy for many spouses and others closest to the vet. It's not easy to feel replaceable or disposable. The overall coping skills identified in the final chapter of this book may prove helpful.

At the core of all healing, of course, is understanding. Many spouses speak of trying to penetrate the Hanoi Connection by understanding the bond among vets. The journey to understanding is detailed especially well in the story of one combat vet's wife.

She tells of sitting on the living room sofa with her husband and paging through his yearbook from boot camp. Though married for several years, this was the first time he had brought out the yearbook. They sat there for hours; sometimes her husband paged quickly, and at other times slowly. Occasionally, he stopped to study a page intently.

At all times, the wife eyed her husband curiously. He pointed to this person, that person, talked of this happening and that happening. Sometimes he chuckled to himself, obviously remembering a funny incident or joke. "Wonder where that guy is today ... That guy got his head blowed off in 'Nam. Happened right away ... This guy was a real nut; funniest person you'd ever want to know ..."

At the moment of realization, the woman was consumed with horror and sadness. "My God," she cried, "this is my husband's high school yearbook! His life is unfolding before me!" The realization hit her not so much for the experiences he had lived, but for the experiences he had not. He had never known the silliness of just being a teen-ager – dating, drinking wine in the cemetery, making out in the back seat of a car. She gasped at the huge void in her husband's life! Fred Gusman further explains this void:[5]

Some veterans might feel safe being with other veterans because they are veterans – not that they share a common experience; what we find is they don't. In reality, they all may have been to Vietnam and seen some terrible things and maybe participated in some terrible things, but how they were affected is independent of each other... The reality is that trauma is an individual experience and a violation of one's identity, a violation of Self.

Sometimes you try to re-live something. You might have lost somebody. You meet somebody who was also in Vietnam and become attached. Your attachment is based on something that doesn't necessarily exist right now, but is past, unfulfilled, unfinished business.

The yearbook brought out a lot of realizations for the wife. What was especially clear to her now was that her husband's preoccupation with vet friends was based on some unfinished business of the past. He was obviously trying to recapture something – some kind of feeling, belief or state of being – that he had lost during the war and during the years since.

Understanding the Hanoi Connection made little difference in the wife's ability to cope, however. And the realization did not improve the overall quality of her life. She continues to view her husband's preoccupation with the war and his war buddies as a wedge between them, and sometimes as a convenient excuse to run from present-day realities.

Patty is gentler in her assessment of the Hanoi Connection. The wife of a Vietnam vet who saw an unusual amount of combat, Patty in fact welcomes her husband's buddies. During bad times, she encourages him to reach out in any way that makes him feel comfortable. She generously allows him to make long-distance calls to vet friends around the country. And she never stands in his way when he wants to venture out alone to visit a friend in another state. She is unique in her willingness, too, to open up the couple's home to friends who wish to visit. Short or long stays, Patty is fine with either.

Patty is liberal in her view of war buddies because it is they, she believes, who inspire and even keep her husband alive. She has no desire to break the bond among them; in fact, "it can't be broken," she claims.

Patty sees the alternative as so much worse. If vets do not cope with their pain in some way, as through each other, "they will destroy themselves." She cites self-medication or even suicide as real possibilities. Psychotherapist Kathryn Berg gives this view of war buddies:[6]

It wasn't the battle that they saw or their buddy blowing up. It's the incredible guilt they felt or the helplessness, or the rage or the devastation to the meaning in their being. It was the evil they faced. It destroyed a basic belief that they had about life, and that's what got buried inside and what we call the existential crisis.

I think trauma diminishes people's value in themselves in some way ... Trauma separates them from the rest of humanity. It makes them feel somehow defective. And so the reason for needing their buddies is partly to somehow still feel human.

Patty sums up the essence of the Hanoi Connection as the quest for comfort and safety. "Vets are so desperately searching for a place to be safe." In her heart, Patty knows she cannot provide that safe haven for her husband. But she knows where he can find it – with other vets.

CHAPTER SIX

THE FIREFIGHT AT HOME: LIFE AS A "BOUNCING BETTY"

PTSD AND FEAR

Dear Journal,

Geez, he kept things hoppin' around here today! Seems like we were all runnin' around like chickens with our heads cut off. Wish he'd learn to slow down a bit.

Sometimes it gets so noisy, I can't hear myself think. Would be nice to have some peace and quiet. The only time he rests is when he sleeps, and then he doesn't rest all that well, either. Would love to have the house to myself today. Alone ...

(Exhausted) Me

THE RUNAWAY TRAIN

The time was 10 minutes to 4 in the afternoon. Barbara and her two young children looked at the clock, knowing that at any moment the peace of the day would be shattered.

That's when Barbara's husband would be home from work. The "runaway train," she describes. "He'd get in the house and just ram around. It was scary. Didn't want to be around him."

The scenario was played out over and over, each afternoon for years. Dad comes home, everyone splits. Eventually, the family stopped eating meals together (the kids didn't want to be around), and everyone in the household walked on eggshells. No one wanted to set Dad off; no one wanted the screaming and the confrontations.

Like many other vets with Posttraumatic Stress Disorder, Barbara's husband is combat-ready at all times. Ready for deployment and ready for action! Trouble is, the "action" occurs within the family. The adrenaline rush that served him so well in war is out-of-place and even destructive in civilian life.

"Some veterans say they're hooked on adrenaline," writes Patience Mason, author and the wife of a vet with PTSD (*Recovering from the War,* Penguin Books, 1990). "Life has never been as exciting as it was in Vietnam, but they constantly try to replace that excitement with new turmoils, traumas, and catastrophes."[1] For vets high on the kind of adrenaline rush they experienced in war, chaos is more normal than peace; the rush gives them a sense of being in control.

(Barbara, like other spouses who hear their vet's war stories, can't believe to this day how her husband survived the rush of his combat experiences. His job as a bodyguard drew constant enemy fire, and he survived many near-death experiences. Once, the tree he was sitting on got shot up; the shell hit and split the branches right above him, but the base – where he was sitting – was spared. Another time he got drunk, fell off a hotel roof in Bangkok and landed on a car. Barbara shakes her head: "I can't imagine anyone going to Vietnam and coming back alive.")

To re-experience the adrenaline rush of yesterday, vets create present-day crises and chaos in many ways. Their thoughts race, race, race, just like their actions. There's an impulsiveness and uncertainty to living with them. Though the specifics differ from home to home, the mood is always the same. Families use terms like "living on a powder keg," "all hell breaking loose" and the "crisis syndrome" to describe the kind of high-pitched intensity of their lives. After years of living with her combat vet, one wife sums it up this way: "His chaos is so normal for me."

Families agree that one of toughest parts of living with PTSD is the unpredictability of it all. They tire of the constant crises, real or imagined, that set their lives so apart from others. A common lament is "Why is my life is so confusing?" Loved ones never know what will set the vet off, and when and where the explosion will occur.

STOP THE WORLD, I WANT TO GET OFF!

For Sarah, the most peaceful time of the day is late in the evening, after her husband has trailed off for a couple hours of sleep. Though his combat nightmares keep him awake most of the night, he does manage to rest a little.

What Sarah relishes most about these late nights is the total peace. The absolute quiet. She uses the time well to collect her thoughts, do a little journaling and organize the next day. What a contrast to the hours when her husband is awake! He has the annoying habit of keeping things stirred up, particularly with the two dogs. He loves his dogs but enjoys teasing them so they growl and bark constantly. "The barking drives me nuts," Sarah admits. "I don't know why he can't just hold the dogs and enjoy them. He's got to keep them running around, jumping on furniture. Everything is so noisy when he's around."

Cheryl's household is noisy and riled up most of the time, too. But her husband's technique is a lot more subtle. He likes to get a rise out of people, or to pit one person against the other. He's a master at button-pushing and sarcasm. "He'll make comments like: 'Nice dress. Did you buy it at the Goodwill?'" Cheryl hates how he always works her up, and then ends with a simple, "just kidding."

Sometimes the vet needs a little help from inanimate objects. Sometimes he needs just the right prop to bring on the adrenaline rush.

Maureen blames the family TV set for making life with her vet husband so miserable. What she remembers most about her marriage is the constant blast of the TV, day and night. Maureen found sleep to be impossible under those conditions; her health eventually failed and she had to get out.

Sarah tells of her husband's run-ins with the neighborhood grocery cart. Early in their marriage, she and her husband grocery shopped together. But it didn't take long for Sarah to decide to go it alone. "I hate shopping with a passion," she says, "But going with him was like being in war. He used the cart like a weapon." She tells of him crashing into corners – and people – and taking sharp turns. "It was just awful. Eventually, someone was going to get hurt." The only thing Sarah misses is her husband's swiftness. She laughs: "BANG! BANG! BANG! We were in and out of the store, just like that. I never knew what hit me!"

For some vets, the perfect vehicle for an adrenaline rush is just that – a vehicle. The family car is the vet's weapon, shiny and big and very dangerous.

Patty describes riding with her vet husband as similar to "riding with a demolition guy," headed down the freeway at lightning speed! It's darn scary, she confesses. And even when her husband hands her the keys, he doesn't really let her drive; he grabs the steering wheel and coaches her the entire time.

Barbara tells of her daughter's scary rides with Dad. After one particular incident, her daughter came back petrified. The two had gone shopping, when Dad got mad and accelerated to 80 miles an hour. To this day, the girl refuses to get into the car if Dad is behind the wheel.

Dangerous jobs and dangerous hobbies sometimes get the adrenaline juices flowing. Cindy is convinced that her husband sought jobs in construction to be in high-stress, dangerous situations. He enjoyed it all, she says, the high scaffolds and power tools. He further fed the rush by working additional jobs. "It was a busy, busy time," she recalls. To be part of the whirlwind, Cindy worked right alongside her husband.

Cheryl is convinced that her husband had a similar motive when he chose his job as an electrician. There's nothing more dangerous, she claims, than working around electric wires (her husband has had several on-the-job mishaps, in fact). She also blames his habit of jumping from job to job on his need to keep things hoppin'.

What Kevin remembers most vividly about his stepdad is that "he can't sit down, can't sit down and read a book, for example." A Vietnam vet with three tours to his credit, the man has to be moving, and has to be around people on the move. In contrast, Kevin enjoys a more sedentary lifestyle. "I'm an avid reader," he says. His most enjoyable moments are relaxing with a good science fiction book.

When the two lived together, their pastimes clashed. "My stepdad wanted me to do things like jog with him every day for five miles. But I preferred to read a book. He didn't even approve of my choice of books. He was always saying, 'Keep your body active, not your mind.'" Kevin only shakes his head.

The desire to feed the body, not the mind, is exactly what many loved ones feel is at the heart of PTSD. They say the vet's desire to run from the past causes him to stir up things in the present. It's only natural that he set fires, so he can busy himself putting them out. If he ever does stop to read that book or catch his breath, he might have time to think ... and remember.

FEAR, ANXIETY AND PANIC

For their part, experts attribute many of the vet's behaviors to fear. According to Dr. Aphrodite Matsakis, author and PTSD expert, "The root of PTSD is a fear of loss – of personal annihilation, death, or dismemberment, or of losing others" (*Vietnam Wives*, Woodbine House, 1988).[2] Dr. Stephen Barton, psychiatrist at the VA Hospital in Minneapolis, Minnesota, explains that fear may appear in many ways:[3]

Often families will note that patients will go into periods of hyperactivity or panic and this is somewhat perplexing to them. Early in the day, the veteran might seem to be calm and then suddenly, without notice, he is calling over the countryside – that is, calling other veterans, maybe even in distant states – or he may engage in other behaviors such as having so much anxiety that he has to go to the bathroom frequently. He might pee in his pants or defecate unexpectedly. He might be seen to actually change color of his skin and become tearful.

There are actually two reasons for these behaviors, Dr. Barton explains. First, many vets with PTSD also develop other disorders including Generalized Anxiety Disorder or Panic Disorder. With Generalized Anxiety, the vet is in a general state of continuous anxiety, which is "part and parcel of PTSD in the sense that hyperarousal is a core symptom." With Panic Disorder, "there's an overwhelming, sudden onset of anxiety which affects all the various physical parts of the body such as the physiological functions of the body – i.e., rapid breathing or the activation of the gastrointestinal tract, causing the need to go to the bathroom. There might be jiggling of the hands and arms or twitching."[4]

(The American Psychiatric Association describes the victim of panic disorder as suffering sudden "intense, overwhelming terror for no apparent reason." The fear is accompanied by symptoms including sweating, heart palpitations, hot or cold flashes, trembling, feelings of unreality, choking or smothering sensations, shortness of breath, chest discomfort, faintness, unsteadiness, tingling, fear of losing control, dying or going crazy. "Often, people suffering a panic attack for the first time rush to the hospital, convinced they are having a heart attack" (reprinted with permission from *Anxiety*

Disorders. Copyright 1988 American Psychiatric Association).[5] For a complete description, refer to the *Diagnostic and Statistical Manual of Mental Disorders*, published by the association as a handbook for clinicians.)

The second reason for the vet's hyperactive behavior is that he can be triggered "back into a very primitive state of feeling the fear of death" says Dr. Stephen Barton.[6] Anything can be a trigger – the sound of a helicopter, airplane or firecracker. Sometimes the vet can even flash back to combat.

Experts refer frequently to the vet's hypervigilance and startle reaction. Always on the lookout for life-threatening situations, even in peacetime, the vet reacts quickly to his surroundings. He hits the deck when a plane flies overhead, or he dives under furniture when someone enters the room.

There are many ways in which the vet tries to decrease his anxieties. He may engage in compulsive or repetitive activities, such as calling people, checking door locks for safety or working excessively. Or he may participate in high-risk activities, such as driving too fast or picking a fight with the biggest bruiser in the bar. "All of these are attempts to gain some sense of control over the environment, some sense that (he) can bring under control those feelings which seem to be so pervasive and out-of-control," Dr. Stephen Barton continues.[7] Unfortunately, the fear sometimes turns to rage, which presents a whole new set of problems. Rage is one of the reasons why vets beat their partners or engage in extremely dangerous activities. (The stories of families living with PTSD and anger are presented in Chapter Seven.)

To further complicate the picture, Panic Disorders may be accompanied by agoraphobia, defined by the American Psychiatric Association as "anxiety about, or avoidance of, places or situations from which escape might be difficult (or embarrassing) or in which help may not be available in the event of having a Panic Attack or panic-like symptoms" (reprinted with permission from the *Diagnostic and Statistical Manual of Mental Disorders, Fourth Edition*. Copyright 1994 American Psychiatric Association).[8] With agoraphobia, victims often feel like they cannot leave their homes.

Besides agoraphobia, panic is often associated with depression, alcohol and drug abuse, and suicidal tendencies. "Recent studies in the general population have suggested that suicide attempts are more common among people who have panic attacks than among those who do not have a mental disorder" (U.S. Department of Health and Human Services).[9]

In summary, the vet and his family may face not only PTSD, but additional – and often very serious – problems as well. The picture can become very complex.

THE MILIEU OF FEAR

I am a Nam vet,
An anxious person,
An intense person,
A humorous person at times to
relieve stress.
An angry person,
A giving person,
A very stressed person.
      – Bill, Vietnam vet with two tours

When Bill's wife read his poem, she, too became anxious and stressed. She wondered, "How am I supposed to deal with someone who has these kinds of problems?" She found herself dwelling on the enormousness of his pain. She became afraid, equally so for herself.

As with other symptoms and behaviors of PTSD, the vet's fears can also be picked up by his family. What results is a cycle: The vet makes his family afraid; the family's fears feed back into the vet, who becomes even more fearful. According to Dr. Stephen Barton the result is "a general milieu of fear in the family – the children are afraid, the mother is afraid, the parents are afraid and the (vet) is afraid."[10]

Family members caught in this milieu of fear do many things to make themselves and the vet feel better. They may participate in the tiptoe syndrome, tiptoeing around the vet to keep him calm and under control. In households that practice tiptoeing, "Mom and kids have secrets" explains Kathryn Berg, psychotherapist.[11] They keep things from Dad to avoid riling him up.

If the vet is angry or acting out, the family may again tiptoe around him, or they may respond with equal anger. Either circumstance is painful; the family care-takes and avoids, or it strikes back in some way. Unfortunately, the cycle of fear in the family often becomes a cycle of violence, substance abuse and other harmful behaviors.

Sometimes families react to the *possibility* of violence or other harmful behaviors. They are especially fearful if such behaviors have occurred in the past. As Kevin says of his stepdad, "He was not really all that violent. But you always knew the possibility was there ..."

For Richard's family, the night he held a gun to his temple is one they will never forget. Though he tried this stunt only once, his general broody nature makes his family feel it could happen again. They live in constant terror of a repeat performance.

With a vet's startle reaction, family members often come face to face with unexpected anger and violence. It is this quality of being unexpected that has the greatest impact. Those who have felt the wrath of startle reaction learn never to tangle with it again.

Cheryl tells of her shock the first time she played a joke on her Vietnam vet husband. The incident occurred right after they were married. "I hid behind the door and surprised him," she recalls. "His reaction *really* scared me!"

Kevin tells of getting a similar response from his stepdad. "He was in the garage," Kevin says. "I opened the door and scared him to death. He yelled at me. It wasn't the reaction I had expected."

And Barbara recounts the story about her husband when he had just returned from Vietnam. He was living at home, when his sister tried to wake him up. She managed to wake him up all right – and to get herself knocked clear across the room! To this day, the poor girl is astounded by what happened to her.

Many families respond to the milieu of fear by getting caught up in the rush of things – the crisis of the moment, or the whirlwind of activities. One vet's wife talks of her life as an endless round of "things that gotta get done." Her routine never changes. Each day she gets up, goes to work, comes home, spends the evening undoing all the troubles her husband caused during the day, does her nighttime chores, goes to bed. The next day, and all days to come, she repeats the exact same schedule. The woman is happy about her nonstop busyness. She explains, "If I ever stop to think, I'll only get angry and afraid."

Some families like to add fuel to the fire by taking on other people's crises as well. The wife of one combat vet describes how she often takes on all the problems of other vets' wives. As if her own problems weren't enough, she finds herself meddling in everyone else's affairs. She takes people in, drives them around, takes them to dinner, etc. Psychotherapist Kathryn Berg explains the reason why many families living with PTSD get caught in such emotional intensity:[12]

Families tend to get involved in all these crises outside of the family as a way of distracting ... it's also a way of feeling you can take some action, to get involved in something as opposed to sitting back and feeling kind of passively helpless.

Families caught up in the rush of problems, theirs and others', eventually feel like life is a merry-go-round. 'Round and 'round she goes, never stopping or letting up. The crises and diversionary activities make the spouse, children and others living with PTSD feel like rats in a maze, using up energy and getting absolutely nowhere.

The milieu of fear may have another dramatic effect on families. Members may find themselves unexpectedly fearful, even terrorized, and they may even develop physical reactions. Over time, the physical reactions may actually develop into physical problems.

Shannon grew up in a home with lots of crises and chaos. Her Vietnam vet father did a lot to stir things up. He often targets her with his anger:

The adrenaline starts pumping pretty hard sometimes. You just got to let it go 'cuz you keep butting heads and it's not getting any better. If someone's arguing, don't feed into that fire and it'll die. That's what I've learned to do. Me and my dad are exactly alike. We've always tried our whole lives to get the last word in, and now I've just learned to let it go so he has nothing to come to me about.

In spite of her efforts to "let it go," Shannon still feels the effects of her father's behavior. "It's frustrating. I get lost, confused and angry," she says.

Terrorized and paranoid – this is how the wife of one combat vet describes the impact of PTSD on her daughter. The girl, now a young teen, was especially traumatized when her parents separated while she was in elementary school. Her mom tells of the girl's hysteria when dropped off at school. Though mystified at first by her daughter's behavior, the mom eventually came to understand the reason. "She was worried something would happen to me while driving, and she would have to live with her dad." The thought of living with Dad was so horrible the girl could not function. She had to be reassured that alternative arrangements had been made – she would never, under any circumstances, have to live with her father.

Sarah blames her overall exhaustion, overeating and physical ailments on her husband's PTSD and Panic Disorder. She says the panic wears especially hard on her sense of well-being. She almost mimics her husband's symptoms and behaviors – the trembling; short, choppy breaths; chest pains; unsteady walk; and fear of dying.

Mabel has weathered her husband's traumas from World War II for more than 50 years. She is staunch in maintaining that his nervous condition has had little effect on her. Throughout the years, she has successfully raised the couple's children and maintained the home, all the while providing great support to her husband. Today, she continues to care for his needs and continues to respond to his nervous hyperactivity. She remains "on guard," in her words, or always available when he needs her.

Asked if there's anything she would like to do for herself, Mabel responds: "Someday I wish he could go someplace for a week or two and leave me alone." She remembers having a few free hours when her daughter filled in and took her husband to a doctor appointment. "I sat in that chair until they came home. I was so relaxed, so myself."

Mabel does not readily admit to having physical problems from living with her husband's nervousness for so many years. "I've been pretty lucky so far," she says. There's "just this nervous condition, they think I might have now ..."

Still, she remains devoted to her husband's needs, ever mindful that he's in the next room and could need her at any moment.

CHAPTER SEVEN

CHARLIE, RAGE AND THE FAMILY

PTSD AND ANGER

Dear Journal,
Today was very bad. He hit me for the first time. Yah, there have been other close calls. But today he actually balled his fist and hit me. Think I'll have a black eye from it. Probably can't go to work tomorrow.

Wonder where all this anger comes from. Can't be from me – don't do anything to bring it on. Guess I'll just have to try harder. Hope things settle down.

Can't believe he's the same sweet, gentle man I married. There's like this little monster inside ...

Me (with a black eye)

ASSAULTS ON THE HOMEFRONT

Cindy had no time to collect her thoughts. She had to leap back, jump out of bed and be ready to defend herself. Her husband's assaults had begun.

He was standing there again, in the middle of the night, screaming within an inch of her nose. What started as an occasional affront became a nightly horror. Cindy was never quite sure what triggered his anger, or why he directed it at her. She saw herself as completely innocent. Always the dutiful wife, hard-working breadwinner, attentive mother, gracious host, good housekeeper – there was just no reason for these emotional outbursts.

Over time, Cindy learned to deal with the fear that gripped her during these nightly ordeals. She learned to control her own anger; for if she ever showed it back, she feared, the cycle would never stop. And she learned to sleep lightly, one eye in the direction of the door. Always in the back of her mind was the thought that her husband could kill her.

The emotional outbursts intensified. The screaming got louder, and the threat of violence more menacing. Cindy's husband never did strike her, but she felt the possibility was always there. Exhausted and distraught, Cindy began acting out; her husband recalls the time she came at him with a knife, pushing on his chest.

Eventually, the house was engulfed in hate and rage, each side consumed with acts of revenge. The looks, how they hurt. The words, how they stung. Cindy began showing severe physical symptoms of stress. She occasionally had chest pains and hair loss, and suffered short-term memory problems. During a couple trips to the grocery store, she completely forgot where she was.

In a culminating event, Cindy's husband pulled out one of his shotguns. Through a mutual friend, he let it be known that if Cindy came home from work, he would shoot her.

Cindy was sure he meant it. For several days, she hid out at a local motel, concealing her whereabouts from everyone. Looking around the cheap motel room she asked, "What am I doing here? How did things get so out of hand?" Her glorious marriage to a Vietnam vet hero had deteriorated into a shabby nightmare.

The couple divorced. Cindy made a new life for herself but often ponders the past. She tries to come to grips with the intense anger that so defined her marriage. "It was actually always there," she says, "even in the early days." She recalls being married for only a little while when her husband balled his fist and hit the dashboard. "That should have been a warning sign," she says, shaking her head.

Her husband, on the other hand, continues to brood about the bitch that ruined his life. The seething anger and hate are still evident in his voice.

Anger is a common undercurrent in homes of vets with PTSD. One vet describes himself as "angry all the time, floating in and out of rage." His wife agrees with the assessment. "He's never truly happy," she says; "He's always got an attitude problem." She describes his moods as rotating between crabby and cynical, and out of control, screaming and throwing things at her and the family pets. "The only time he loosens up is when he's got a beer in his hand."

Her husband grins, "I've killed a lot of toasters in my day." His outbursts, though erratic, are extremely damaging. The house bears witness; there are holes in the walls, chips in the bathroom tile, torn wallpaper and deep gouges in the furniture. The man's wife hates the aftermath. She also fears that one day the rage will be directed at her instead of inanimate objects. She shudders at the time when he struck out against her kitty. She quickly caged the poor animal and put him in the basement for protection. Out of sight, out of mind, she figured.

Besides house damage, the woman also faces her husband's remorse. "I never really want to hurt my own stuff," he cries. "But I just can't seem to help it."

Shannon, the daughter of a Vietnam vet, knows all too well the pain of growing up in a house brimming with anger, fear and violence. Through the years, her dad has often struck out at her. She knows the feel of his hands around her throat.

But one image plays over and over in her mind. "I was like three or four," she says. "I'll never forget it. I heard my mom screaming. I crawled out of my crib and went out to the living room. My mom was laying in the closet. Dad was standing over her with a belt in his hand. That was something that stayed with me my whole life. I've always been afraid of him. I wish that fear wasn't there."

Shannon describes her dad's rage as falling into seven-year cycles. On the seventh year, he explodes. "It's coming to the point where he's going to explode and lose it again. It's getting really close." Shannon fears the next few months of life.

As damaging as the physical assaults are the verbal assaults that consume many households with PTSD. Sarah's husband, a two-tour Vietnam vet, does not hurt her physically. Rather, he assaults her with endless verbal tirades. At times she's a "bitch, whore and slut." At other times, she's "stupid, lazy and no good." Ironically, Sarah says, she's the one who provides, keeps up the house and handles all financial affairs. She also hints at being a virgin when she met her husband. "The slutty names really don't fit me," she claims.

And then there's the "F" word. The infamous "F" word. Sarah is furious by her husband's use of the word all the time. "He uses it over and over again, especially when he's mad at me. I grew up in a conservative house, and this kind of language bothers me. I don't care if he used it in Vietnam. This is his home." Still, her husband continues to swear at her, and continues to use the "F" word freely.

Once during one of these name-calling episodes, Sarah could no longer bear to be around her husband. He had already rousted her out of bed and demanded she get out of the house. Sarah promptly got dressed (though it was only four in the morning), hopped in her car and drove around until it was time to go to work. By the time she got to the office, she had already put in a full day.

Though the erratic outbursts of anger and the horrible language scare and offend her, Sarah claims to be more bothered by her husband's downer attitude. An upbeat, professional woman, she is mystified by her husband's hate-all attitude. "He can't stand life," she states. "It's hard to be with someone who is so untrustworthy of every situation and every person. His nonstop complaining grates on my nerves." Sarah struggles with her husband's belief that he has been shortchanged in life. She doesn't understand why he believes the world owes him a living. "I'm not kidding you," she says, "when I turn my back, he steals the tip we leave for the waitress."

Sometimes, Sarah's husband screams for an entire day about the terrible state of his existence. Attacks like these can last well into the evening. Sarah describes these incidents:

He screams at me because he has such a boring life ... He screams at me because it's supposed to rain the next day and he had planned to go fishing ... He screams at me because the crunchy peanut butter is gone and now what's he supposed to eat. When I remind him that I'm not responsible for things like the weather, he gets madder still. I guess I'm the one within earshot, so he figures I'm supposed to just sit and listen. It's like he punishes me for being his wife. When is he going to understand that marriage doesn't mean being abused?

Sarah is astounded to know that her husband DOESN'T THINK HE HAS ANY ANGER, even when he's screaming.

Cheryl describes her husband as a "victim person, used and abused by everyone." She is disgusted at how he actually brings on the problems himself. Like the couple's money woes, a direct result of his wild spending sprees. "He buys everything, mostly dumb things we don't need." Cheryl cites the time he bought a horse instead of fixing up the hobby farm.

Feeling victimized, Cheryl's husband makes further victims out of those around him. He targets the helpless, including his own son, ill from a devastating disease. "My husband can't stand to see anything that's a sign of weakness. My son's disease makes him appear weak. In fact, he missed an entire year of school." Cheryl shakes when she thinks of how the anger nearly destroyed the young boy.

Ruth's husband is a mild-mannered World War II vet whose occasional outbursts of anger are directed at the entire outside world. "People just don't respect the war and those who fought it," he announces. "People don't understand why we were there, what went on; they don't teach it, they don't observe it," he says, pounding his fist. One year on Dec. 7, he was driven to near rage when the metro papers failed to carry stories about Pearl Harbor Day. He called the editors, only to find "they really didn't understand why I was calling!" He denounces the nation's education system for not teaching his view of American history. "We don't teach where we came from, who we are and where we're going."

Ruth is calm through it all. She is attentive but has obviously heard her husband's viewpoints many times before.

Sandra's husband is a veteran of both the Korean and Vietnam Wars. A mild-mannered man, he visibly loves his wife. The two enjoy a close, tranquil relationship.

But the relationship has a crack, one that drives the man to hysterical verbal attacks. Normally speaking in whisper tones, he raises his voice in disgust when referring to Sandra's 17-year-old son. The house seethes with tension when talk of the boy begins.

"I have a son from a previous marriage," Sandra explains, "and there's a lot of anger and rage against him. The bottom line is that my husband doesn't feel he should have to raise him when he has a lot of problems of his own." Lately, the boy has been in trouble with the law, fueling the problems. As Sandra sees it, the only solution is for her son to move out when he turns 18.

Sandra is sad, but philosophical about her husband's misdirected anger. Like other vets, she says, he hates all Asians. Her son is half Korean.

The restraining orders, the presence of knives and guns, the stalking in the night, the screaming and stomping that could blow a house apart, the personal attacks to pride and safety, the ranting and raving about "this rotten world" – families of vets have endured it all.

TRAINED TO KILL ...

Tom is a Vietnam veteran. And he's darn angry. His anger spreads from here to there, and it's as wide as the ocean.

"I'm angry at not being able to save the little children," he moans. "When you had to burn a village, and shoot the children" – this makes Tom especially angry.

He's angry at the government. "Most of what upsets me is our government," he says, "not so much the enemy." He's angry over the way the government forced him to fight the war, and angry at the government's treatment of grunts, or front-line guys like himself (they were more concerned with the lives of officers, he claims).

And Tom's angry at the treatment he got when he came home. Stranded in California, he couldn't even hitch a ride in uniform. He's angry at everybody for not understanding and for not giving him the respect he deserves.

Tom's feelings echo those of many Vietnam vets, who, in fact, appear to have lots of reasons to be angry. According to Dr. Arthur Blank, Jr., formerly of the DAV Readjustment Counseling Service the Vietnam experience left lots of scars.

In his manuscript, *Anger in Vietnam Veterans,* Dr. Blank details 30 reasons why Vietnam vets are angry.[1] The reasons are varied. There are the physical scars – being wounded or maimed, or getting cancer from Agent Orange. There are reasons of loss – loss of friends and the innocence of youth. There are reasons of politics – the divisiveness and deceptions of the war and the policies of those in charge.

The 30 reasons are numbing. No wonder so many Vietnam vets are boiling pots. No wonder they're so damn irritable. Though vets of other wars may not share the exact prescription for anger, they, too, have their own reasons to be angry.

There are several tricky aspects to PTSD anger, making it difficult to understand. First, it often covers up something else. What the vet and his family see, may not actually be the problem. Psychotherapist Kathryn Berg explains:[2]

> *Soldiers aren't allowed to be afraid. Soldiers have to camouflage their fear and PTSD veterans camouflage their fear very often with anger. And the family then – in reaction to that – misunderstands the symptoms that are covering up the fear. The anger is misinterpreted because the fear doesn't appear as fear.*

The other tricky thing about PTSD anger, Dr. Blank continues, is that it springs from the past but disrupts the present.[3] What appears to be a modern-day crisis may actually be founded in events that happened years, even decades, ago. Reminders of the combat situation can occur in the present through "triggers." For example, a vet can be triggered by riding in an elevator playing music from the '60's. The music reminds him of Vietnam, and suddenly he becomes irritated about a present-day situation, such as unpaid bills.

Combat PTSD can also make people appear to be enemies when they are not or situations appear to be problems when they are not, Blank explains.[4] Those living around the vet often remark about his lack of proportion. He lets big issues slide and stews over small ones. Spouses share common stories about their husbands' battles with mechanical things. "There he goes, in one of his fits again," cries the wife of one combat vet who frequently tangles with the family lawn mower. "He's throwing it down the sidewalk, all because there's a little screw missing." She marvels at his frustration over fixable problems and at his negligence over bills and other biggies.

The wife asks her husband, when he finally calms down, "Why is it that you blow things out of proportion like that?" Her husband replies that he holds a different view about what is a big problem versus a small problem. He also warns his wife that her nonchalance towards the issue at hand makes him angrier still. "It's the little inconveniences that drive me crazy," he explains. "Besides," he continues, "it's the little things that got you killed in 'Nam." He also admits that his own impatience doesn't help, but blames the impatience on PTSD. The wife shakes her head; this time, it is she who is frustrated.

Anger is also tied in with the phenomenon of survival guilt. It is popularly known that vets who made it home when their buddies did not have all sorts of feelings. Anger is one of them. Over and over they ask, "Why wasn't it me? Why didn't I get hit that day?" Often, the questions continue through life, like an endless movie.

Anger is tied in with other feelings like depression and remorse. PTSD expert and author Aphrodite Matsakis offers this explanation in her book, *Vietnam Wives* (Woodbine House, 1988):[5]

While the Vietnam vet is often portrayed as a violent individual, this image is false. In reality, the vet who suffers primarily from PTSD more accurately suffers from impacted, or suppressed anger, and consequently, from depression, which is often anger turned inward. When the vet is no longer able to keep a lid on his anger, however, rage reactions do occur. Yet, unless the veteran suffers from problems in addition to his PTSD, his rage reactions may be intermittent and followed by remorse and even greater efforts to suppress his anger.

Loved ones who live with the cycle of rage and remorse refer to this as the "Jekyll-Hyde Syndrome." They speak of the unpredictability of the vet's rage, and how quickly it can be brought on. Many also speak of the periods of remorse, when everything looks like it will be better. That's the time of apologies, candy and flowers. That's the time when loved ones break down and take back the repentant vet. Though the Jekyll-Hyde Syndrome can be broken, often it is not. (Vets themselves admit to being afraid of their Jekyll-Hyde personalities. They fear hurting others during their outbursts. One vet tells his wife to leave the house when he begins to feel badly. "I don't want to be responsible for what I might do.")

The military machine itself contributes to the family's problems with anger and violence. Trained to be killers in a dehumanizing environment, vets return home to find their training inappropriate in civilian life. The vets' anger "at the system that abused them can lead to a you-owe-me-attitude" (Patience Mason, *Recovering from the War*).[6] This attitude further results in self centeredness and relentless demands on others.

Cindy, for one, is certain that her husband's aggression towards her – particularly the way he used to wake her within an inch of her nose – is very much due to his military training. She is sure he would have been very happy had she quit her job and devoted all her time to him. Though dutiful and attentive, she refused to totally subordinate herself.

With all its complexities, deceptions and relationships to the past, is it any wonder the vet's anger appears so hit-and-miss? Is it any wonder that it leaves those around him mystified and wondering, "What did I do?"

WEATHERING THE STORM

It's not easy to stay calm or silent when you're being called dumb, a lousy housekeeper and a failure in life. So says the wife of one Vietnam combat vet. Still, she endures the one-hour screaming attacks in her face because the alternative is worse. Worse things will happen to her, she predicts, if she gets mad back.

Families weather the storm of their vets' anger and violence in many ways. Some try to ignore the anger altogether. Some try harmful defenses like overeating or taking drugs. Some try to be invisible, hoping their silence will keep away the screaming. And some find no other alternative but to leave.

Some react by expressing their own angers. Sarah is angry about having to "do it all while he's busy talking about the war." Barbara is angry for not having left her vet husband sooner, and now that she has, she is angry that he gets financial compensation for PTSD while she struggles. Shirley is angry about the whole Vietnam War and the unresolved POW/MIA situation. Cheryl is angry that her husband is either "digging or distant." Doris is angry that her son is just pretending to have PTSD.

Kevin is philosophical about the effects of a lifetime of anger and violence directed at him. Though he has weathered his stepdad's PTSD and battled the demons of drugs, he just can't seem to shake his own pervading cynicism. "The drugs and PTSD have made me doomed to see the bad side of things," he claims. "I'm forever seeing the stupid things that people do."

Vets have many legitimate reasons to be angry. Their loved ones have a few of their own.

CHAPTER EIGHT

WALKING POINT ... ALL NIGHT LONG

PTSD AND SLEEPLESSNESS

Dear Journal,
We've had really sleepless weeks around here lately. Don't think he's slept more than 10 minutes in the past 48 hours. I can't sleep, either. Too hard to rest when he's tossin' and turnin'.

Poor kids haven't slept so well, either. They hear Dad walkin' around all night. Imagine they wonder why he keeps pacing, back and forth. The floor squeaks, too. Even our poor cocker spaniel can't get any rest. Can hardly keep his big brown eyes open.

Somedays I'd like to club him over the bed and make him sleep! I'm afraid if me and the kids shut our eyes, we won't ever want to wake up.

Me (so tired I could die!)

"NOT THE BABIES!"

The screams shatter the peace of the night. "Please, not the babies!" Over and over, Sandra hears her husband's nighttime pleas. "Not the babies!"

There's the dark figure, the one who sneaks into their bedroom to bludgeon them to death. He's carrying something. Not sure what it is. Sandra's husband cries out in terror. She tries to comfort him.

I didn't want to shake him or touch him in that condition, so I slowly tried talking to him. "Honey, it's time to wake up, time to get up." He slowly came out of it. That was the worst time.

Ron and Doris are awakened every night to the sound of their son's nightmares. It's the eyes, they explain, that triggered the problem nearly a decade ago. For the past 10 years, they have listened to the painful tale of those eyes:

Grandma's dog had to be put to sleep. So our son took the dog to the vet. The dog just looked at him. It must have been a trigger. He remembers the dying man in Vietnam. The man looked up; our son told him he would be OK. The man said, "You're lying." Then he died. The dog gave him that same look.

Bernie still wonders when the nightmares will return to her bed. Her husband's terrors rocked their slumber for several months after his return from the Gulf War:

He'd sit bolt upright and say, "No, get out of here! There's someone here!" He wouldn't shout it, but it was abrupt. I'd say, "There's no one here." And he'd say, "Oh." He'd lay down and I think go back to sleep and I'd be wide awake. Not too long after the first few nights, it appeared he thought I may have been someone coming to get him in bed because he sat up and took a swing and grabbed me. He'd say, "Get out of here, who are you?" It was kind of scary. It didn't happen every night, couple times a week.

During one of the nightmares, Bernie's husband sat up and swung at her with a closed fist. The blow hit her in the shoulder blades, in the lower part of the neck. Though not landing with full force, it caused excruciating, lasting pain.

To this day, Bernie's husband occasionally wrestles with his nighttime memories of war. But the episodes are further and further apart.

SLEEP, NO MORE

For many combat vets, the horrors of war last a lifetime. Over and over, they re-experience these horrors in their sleep – the burning village, the sinking ship, the look in the dying man's eyes.

For most, night is the scariest, the time when they feel most vulnerable. They remember landing on the beaches or fighting in the jungles at night, never knowing for sure who was lying or standing next to them. Many complain of not having a peaceful night's rest since before the war.

Vietnam vets, in particular, complain of terror in the night. They talk of having to be on guard during "set-up time," the hours right around dusk. Most terrifying is early morning, two or three o'clock, when the Viet Cong were most likely to strike. Fearing both the nightmares and their own vulnerability, many actually avoid falling asleep. For them, rest is only a brief cat nap during the day.

But there are many reasons besides nightmares for sleep deprivation among vets. Experts cite the symptoms and behaviors of PTSD – including depression, substance abuse, hypervigilance – which contribute to sleeplessness. Often, the picture is confused. In one common scenario, PTSD disturbs sleep because of nightmares; the disturbed sleep results in depression, which further feeds back into PTSD. The cycle is ongoing and vicious.

Though experts still study the effects of sleeplessness in vets, one thing is certain: It impairs the quality of their life, and that of their loved ones. (Many PTSD treatment programs, such as the National Center for PTSD in Menlo Park, California, examine the physiological aspects of the disorder, including the issue of sleep. The center maintains one of the world's most recognized PTSD sleep study labs.)

SPOUSES AND WALKING POINT

For spouses and children of combat vets, night can also be a time of sleeplessness and terror. They share the vet's nightmares and are ever mindful of the sounds of the dark. They sleep with one eye open, never really falling into deep slumber. For them, every night is like walking point.

Spouses who co-experience the vet's nightmares can actually develop combat nightmares themselves, explains Dr. Arthur Blank Jr.[1] So great is the impact of their vet's dreams, that they, too, have dreams of their own.

For many spouses and loved ones, however, sleeplessness is not due to combat nightmares, at least not their own. More common is the fear of the vet's behaviors at night. Loved ones fear his acting out during dreams, e.g., thinking they are the Viet Cong. Or they fear the consequences of his nightlong drinking binge. Or they fear the guns he pulls out to protect his family and property at night. These are the real nighttime worries of families who live with PTSD. These are the real reasons that spouses, children and even family pets keep a watchful eye in the dark.

Patience Mason, author and wife of a Vietnam combat vet, sums up the impact of sleep deprivation on vets and their loved ones (*Recovering from the War*, Penguin Books, 1990):[2]

If he can't sleep, his behavior will become more and more irrational just because of sleep deprivation. This is natural. Sleep deprivation is a well-known form of torture: Anyone will break under it. Lack of sleep makes a person really hard to live with.

"Really hard to live with" is indeed how families describe their sleep-deprived vet. Not only is he difficult to cope with at night, but he is difficult to live with by day. And family members find themselves difficult to live with, too, as sleeplessness becomes a family pattern. No one in the house thinks clearly, feels good or performs well.

For couples, one of the major outcomes of sleeplessness is lack of intimacy. Often, it's a matter of the vet's hyperalertness; it's hard to hold and caress someone who's jumpy and irritable all the time. But many times intimacy problems develop from the vet's restlessness in bed. Because he just won't go to sleep, the couple is forced to sleep apart. He or she moves to another bed or another bedroom. After all, someone's got to get some rest.

Sarah says she endured years of sleeplessness before taking drastic measures to ensure her own rest. Her husband rotated between screaming and thrashing, and watching TV all night. Either way, Sarah got no sleep. She dodged his swings or was forced to watch the late, late show. Within a couple of years, she knew something had to be done.

Sarah did the extreme. She hired a contractor to finish off a room in the basement. When the room was done, she stated to her husband, simply: "You can have either bedroom, it doesn't matter to me. But we can't sleep together any more." Her husband obliged and chose the basement bedroom. He felt the lower bedroom would be more soundproof, allowing him to pace and keep the TV blaring all night.

Though Sarah does sleep better, she admits to paying a dear price for the separation. She and her husband no longer enjoy the intimacy of their earlier years. "I thought it would be fun to make dates to see each other," she explains. "I thought it would be exciting to ask, 'Your place or mine?' But it hasn't worked out that way. The spark goes out when you don't touch and hold each other every night."

For many spouses, night brings another trauma – staying up to help the vet face his demons. If he's not screaming in terror and needing to come out of a dream, he's fearful of being alone. He may ask, even demand, that loved ones keep him company. Many oblige, forgoing sleep altogether.

Though now sleeping apart from her husband, Sarah complains of occasional vigils in the night. She can always tell before going to bed if her husband is going to have a bad night. If he is, she knows ahead of time that her own rest will be disturbed:

It's really eerie; I'm sleeping, but I feel the presence of someone looking at me. I wake up, and he's staring at me. I've become so used to it that I don't jump or get alarmed any more. Sometimes he speaks to me, and his breath is short and choppy. I can tell he's afraid. I reassure him that all is well, there's nothing to be afraid of. Usually, he accepts my reassurance and goes back down to bed.

Though Sarah has mastered the art of thinking and speaking clearly in her sleep, she complains of overall fatigue and inability to concentrate at work. She is resentful of her husband's intrusions into her slumber, even though she understands why he does it. She marvels at how he can expect her to be good-natured the next day.

For Cindy, helping her former husband face the demons was a full-time job. Added to her full-time day job, Cindy battled fatigue constantly.

It became more and more impossible, she explains, to stay up with her husband past 10, as he requested. She usually made the hard decision to leave him alone and go to bed. But often the picture of him sitting up alone in the dark, shaking with fear, was enough to keep her awake anyway. With time, Cindy broke from exhaustion. She left the marriage to save her health and sanity. Though there were many reasons for the couple's breakup, Cindy says the sleep issue was a big one.

GUARDING THE TOWN

To outsiders – friends, neighbors and strangers – the vet's sleeplessness is a curious phenomenon indeed. They remark about the strange house down the block that always has its lights on. "Doesn't anyone in that house ever go to bed?" they ask. They talk about the guy who takes long walks or drives his motorcycle in the middle of the night. To most of the outside world, the vet and even his family seem to run on a different clock. They seem to have their days and nights all mixed up.

The wife of one combat vet tells what it's like to be out of step with the world's clock. She tells of getting up at four in the morning (her husband makes too much noise for her to sleep) and doing her housecleaning and other chores before the rest of the world is even up. She tells of going to bed right after set-up time, around seven or eight in the evening. And she tells of eating at strange times of the day, having lunch in the morning and supper in the early afternoon.

She also tells of grocery shopping in the middle of the night. It's the best time for her husband, she explains, because he hates crowds and doesn't sleep anyway. She, on the other hand, finds the nighttime shopping trips exhausting and frustrating:

The problem is that the store isn't really geared up for night shoppers. Sure, the doors are open and the "24-hour" sign is flashing, but why do they clutter the aisles with boxes and stock the top shelves on ladders that block your cart? I don't think they really want us here at night.

The residents of one Midwestern neighborhood describe their mixed feelings about the Vietnam vet who lives on their block. His wild flashbacks and other behaviors are of great concern to them. They wonder, "Will he act out against them someday? Are their children safe around him?"

In spite of the behaviors they don't approve of, they report loving the guy's sleepless nights. They tell of feeling comfortable when they see him pace in the dark. They have no fear in turning their lights off because his are always on. They know his vigilance has prevented many break-ins. They feel secure leaving for vacation.

After all, nothing will ever happen to them and their neighborhood. Their Vietnam vet is always up, always on guard and certainly always awake.

CHAPTER NINE

POT, SMACK AND BOOZE

PTSD AND ADDICTIONS

Dear Journal,
  Found some pills in his drawer yesterday. Think he's been taking 'em with beer. No wonder he's so wound up and crazy all the time.
  Think he smoked pot in 'Nam, even shot up some heroin. Didn't think he was doin' drugs any more. Wonder how he's paying for 'em.
  I smoked pot once, too, but didn't like it. Hope the kids don't see him doin' it. Wouldn't want them to start with that stuff. Wouldn't want them to know their dad's a junkie.
  Thought PTSD was bad enough. Now I got to deal with drugs, too.

  Me (wondering when all the problems will end!)

NUMBING THE PAIN

In the midst of the craziness, when there's time to catch their breath, loved ones of vets with PTSD ask the same old question: "Does he drink to forget the war, or does he just think of the war when he's drinking?"

For centuries, this age-old question has baffled loved ones and challenged the experts. Which came first, the PTSD or the drinking? Would he have been an alcoholic without the war? Which do you treat first, the PTSD or the booze? The questions are as mind-numbing as the addictions themselves.

"You do what you have to do to numb out," says one Vietnam combat vet, who uses a combination of prescription drugs and alcohol to numb the pain of his PTSD and panic attacks. "You gotta do what you gotta do to stay alive. It's not that we're stupid. We know this stuff's wrecking our lives. It's just that you're always in this continuous cycle of thoughts ..."

Like the thoughts they're supposed to quell, the addictions themselves become a continuous cycle. The bad memories lead to pills; the pills lead to more bad memories, and on and on and on. With time, the vet's PTSD symptoms and behaviors are amplified by the addictions. What once was a singular (but complex) problem, becomes a problem out of control.

MASKING THE PROBLEM

Alcohol, tobacco and drug use are typical addictions of vets with PTSD. There are others – gambling, food and sex among them. When pursued to excess, any of them can ruin the lives of vets and their loved ones.

Experts have lots to say about PTSD and addictions, particularly about alcohol and drug use, which (along with tobacco) are perhaps most common to vets with PTSD. They speak of "self-medicating," or using drugs and alcohol to medicate away the pain.

Self-medication has always been a part of military life. The drinking, smoking and whoring of soldiers are as legendary images as you'll ever find. And the Vietnam vet – whew! Who hasn't seen the slew of movies with soldiers shooting up in the thick of the jungle? Or smoking pot in the LZ?

The real problem with addictions, the experts claim, is that they confuse the picture of what's actually going on. Drinking and drug use commonly mask the underlying problem of PTSD (experts call the drinking and drug use "masked presentations"). Or sometimes the drinking and drug use are independent of the PTSD; the person may, in fact, have used liquor and drugs before the war. Either way, the vet needs help for both problems.

Tracy describes the complexity of sorting out her husband's PTSD from his alcoholism. She says: "He doesn't drink daily. Consequently, during the week it's easier to judge his moods and understand where they're coming from." But during the weekends, when her husband is drunk from Friday through Sunday, Tracy has a tougher time discerning the real problem. She also notes that her husband drinks mainly within the context of Vietnam; his favorite pastime is to meet up with a war buddy at the local American Legion and drink the night away. So again, she asks, does he drink to forget the war?

The scenario is particularly confusing if the vet is addicted and his PTSD has not been diagnosed Dr. Arthur Blank, Jr., explains:[1]

If the PTSD has not been diagnosed and if it has not been documented that the substance abuse is coming from the PTSD, then the family can have an erroneous picture of what's going on. They may think that the person simply has an alcoholism problem, and it can get very confusing because there may be pressure on the veteran to go to alcohol treatment.

If the alcoholism is coming from PTSD and the treatment program does not deal with both problems, then the alcohol treatment won't work, either.

Sometimes the vet and his loved ones actually prefer to think that alcoholism is the only problem they face. "Alcoholism is more common than PTSD, and PTSD is scary and you don't know what to do with it" says Fred Gusman.[2]

The presence of panic is yet another complication, because panic often goes hand-in-hand with alcoholism. According to Dr. Stephen Barton, persons who suffer panic attacks frequently use alcohol and abusive drugs to "quell the anxiety and fear within them"[3] Added to all the symptoms and behaviors of PTSD, the panic and alcohol/drug use create problems of tremendous proportions!

One of the dark sides of treatment programs for PTSD and panic is the abuse of medications prescribed for those problems. In his quest to find peace, the vet often takes too much prescription medication or takes it in combination with alcohol or street drugs. The intended good is negated.

"What the hell's the difference?" asks one combat vet. "You can drink enough beers to pass out, or you can smoke pot which is illegal, or you can take enough prescribed drugs to be a zombie." He cites the story of one friend who has managed to kick all his habits. "He's off everything, all right, and he's doing *really* well. Now all he does is stare at the wall all day."

Clinicians do indeed have a credibility problem when it comes to convincing the troubled vet of the evils of taking too many drugs. Their typical response is "You've got to be kidding!" Choosing between the hellish nightmares and demons of PTSD and the risk of overmedicating is an easy choice to make.

The result of substance abuse or any other addiction is PTSD gone rampant. "Substance abuse intensifies all of the symptoms of PTSD, and it intensifies the mood swings and the (vets') irrational behavior," explains Kathryn Berg, psychotherapist.[4] What comes out of the irrational behavior, in turn, is anybody's guess. Common responses include spousal abuse, sensation-seeking pursuits or even criminal behavior.

In the short term, alcohol and drugs work pretty well. They help some vets to get much-needed rest. They lift depressed spirits and control bad feelings. But over time, they are a liability, dangerous to health and happiness.

THE ADDICTION MERRY-GO-ROUND

The toll on families living with PTSD and addictions is horrendous. There is no positive portrait; they succumb to addictions themselves, or face years of frustration trying to help the vet kick his habits. Either way, they live a reactive lifestyle, caught up in the wild merry-go-round.

Besides the heavy emotional toll, addictions cause other problems. Financial worries, health problems, social alienation, criminal activity and spousal/child abuse are all real possibilities. For family members who also have addictions, the reactive lifestyle is especially pronounced. Kathryn Berg describes the toll on families:[5]

> *I think of all addictive kinds of behaviors as having an emotional payoff, so that if everyone in the family is trying to avoid painful feelings, substance abuses, eating disorders, gambling addictions, all sorts of addictive, compulsive behaviors are emotional defenses. There are things that people stumble upon as a way of feeling better temporarily; so the veteran feels better temporarily, the family experiments with some of the same things to feel better temporarily to avoid their own emotional pain.*
> *I think children in particular are at high risk for developing addictions, substance abuse problems.*

The temptation is strong for the children of vets with addictions. Shannon remembers picking up her cocaine habit at age 13 because substance abuse was around all the time. "Mom and Dad did it, so why can't I?" Her coke habit sent her in a downward spiral, ending in a baby out of wedlock, more substance abuse including alcoholism, dropping out of school, loss of jobs and even near death. Today, Shannon still battles alcoholism; she spends long days alone, fighting to keep off the bottle.

For Kevin, taking drugs as a teen-ager was the only way to survive life with his stepdad, a three-tour Vietnam vet with his own alcohol and drug problems. Kevin took drugs just to be able to be around the man. "I could get high and tolerate him," Kevin explains. He also began overeating to fill the emotional void created by his stepdad's aloofness.

Though Kevin's stepdad left the family picture years ago, Kevin battled drugs well into his 20's. Clean now except for cigarettes (which he enjoys rolling himself), Kevin blames the addictions – his and his stepdad's – for shaping his entire life. He is most melancholy at the memories of how the addictions "messed up all our family plans."

Spouses of vets with addictions have more choices than their children do. Still, the lure of escapism and the availability of drugs at home make substance abuse all too easy.

Tracy recounts her bouts with alcoholism. She turned to booze, she says, to escape the harshness of her husband's PTSD. "I've known it was no good since I was a kid," she explains. But still the quick fix was there, and she used it. Problem was, each time she sobered up and returned to reality, she faced a bigger mess to clean up. The quick fix only amplified her problems.

For Barbara, drugs were a pastime she shared with her Vietnam vet husband. For years, the two took all sorts of hard drugs together. They popped, smoked, snorted and lived high. But eventually, Barbara decided to kick the drugs and just live the normal life of a wife and mother. She is angry at the time her husband sabotaged her recovery by putting drugs in her food: "He didn't ask me, because he knew I was going to say no. He was already just totally trying to control me. I didn't realize how controlling he really was." The couple divorced, but not before Barbara endured more of the ravages of her husband's PTSD and substance abuse.

Family members not caught up in addictions themselves find their lives caught up in the merry-go-round of their vet's addictions. They plead with him to kick his habit. They schedule their own days around his drinking patterns. They run to the liquor store to buy him a six-pack, and run to the grocery store to pick up his cigarettes. As one non-drinking, non-smoking spouse of a vet says, "I can't believe how much time I spend supporting his bad habits. I'm a slave to his addictions." She cleans up vomit and urine after his binges and helps him into bed.

But mostly loved ones worry about their vet. They worry about his overdoses and worry about his mood changes when he's drunk or high. Their fears are legitimate; while under the influence, his judgment is usually impaired and his inability to control behaviors often leads to actions he would not take during sobriety. As Dr. Stephen Barton explains: "This brings an added problem to the family, because now there is not only the fear of the past

– that is the past combat – but there is the fear of what may happen in the present when (the vet) drinks alcohol."[6]

Sometimes, the efforts and worry of family members pays off. Sometimes they are able to get help for the vet, or are able to support his efforts to get help. For vets willing to kick their addictions, whether on their own or through treatment, life seems a lot more tolerable. The real problems of PTSD are allowed to come out; they and their families set out on the road to recovery.

For many vets and their families, however, the addictions seem unshakable. For whatever reason, the vet refuses to set out on that road to freedom. For families caught in the cycle, life continues to be unbearable.

Patty spent the first 10 years of her marriage angry at her alcoholic husband. "My mother had died of alcoholism," she explains. "I always felt it was a choice that the person has control over. I felt Lonnie (her husband) didn't love me enough, or he would quit."

But Lonnie didn't quit, at least not right away. For years, the couple fought over his drinking. The turning point occurred when Patty left for three months. One night during the separation, she called Lonnie and found him dead-drunk. "I told him, I would not talk with him when he's drunk, but that I would call back in two weeks. And he'd better be sober when I call."

Lonnie was sober when Patty called back. He was even agreeable to entering an alcohol treatment program at the VA Hospital. During her husband's hospital stay, Patty took a major step in requesting that the psychiatric staff conduct further tests to determine if Lonnie had any other problems. The test results came back; Lonnie was diagnosed with PTSD along with alcoholism. The dual diagnosis helped the couple determine an appropriate treatment and follow-up plan. To this day, however, Lonnie frequently succumbs to one or both problems. Patty dreads the occasional alcohol binge, because it only brings out the worst of the PTSD.

Shirley describes what it's like to be the parent of a vet on drugs. She tells of the heartache and guilt and the helplessness of those on the sidelines:

Oh, he was so bad one time. I went out there (to California) and I knew he did drugs and Tom had had a bad trip or something. He was mean and crazy and he cussed me out and all this was my fault. I thought I would die. My heart was broken. I had never seen this side of him and I'd never seen anything like it. All my kids were gentle, respecting. And my heart just broke.

Shirley stuck with her son, Tom, through many more drug episodes, scrapes with the law and broken marriages. Today the two live together, along with Tom's young son, cn a small hobby farm in the Midwest. Their days are fairly peaceful and uneventful, except for Tom's occasional pot smoking.

Shirley still wages a one-woman campaign against her son's drug use. But she finds the efforts futile:

> *Tom smokes a little pot. I know it. He doesn't lie to me. Before, I just had fits, wanted no part of it. You know, I don't need it. One time I found a pot pipe, so I broke it in half and put it on the trash can outside. No – first I just set it down out there so he could see I found it. So the next time I found it, I broke it in half (again) and set it on the trash can. He brought it back in the house and glued it together. The next time I took the hammer and beat the hell out of it and threw it into the trash can!*

For Sarah, life with her vet husband is filled with all sorts of uncertainties. There are the uncertainties that are part of the PTSD package, and there are the uncertainties brought on by her husband's abuse of prescription medications along with alcohol consumption.

"When did my cupboard become a pharmacy?" she asks, quizzically. "When did all this crap find its way onto my shelves?" Sarah stares at the rows and rows of bottles marked Clonazepam, Xanax, Clonidine and Clomipramine. "I have no idea what all this stuff is; all I know is that Bill takes too much of it."

When her husband Bill was first diagnosed with PTSD and Panic Disorder, Sarah tried hard to monitor his medication intake. Each morning, she counted out the little pills – blue ones, white ones, yellow ones – and instructed her husband how many to take and when. Within a few short months, however, she noticed her husband behaving strangely; he was groggy much of the time. She couldn't understand why the doctors prescribed too much medication.

The doctors didn't. Sarah's husband snitched pills behind her back. He took lots of them, mixing them up and even taking them with alcohol. There were days when he took none, and there were days when he took handfuls. He stockpiled supplies all over the house; Sarah found pills in every container – cups, drawers and pockets.

As expected, life became more unpredictable, and Bill more irrational. His wild spending sprees and disappearing acts worried Sarah to death. She worried constantly about money, her job and her health. Finally, she could no longer concentrate at work. She considered leaving Bill. .

One day, the local police department called Sarah at work to tell her that Bill had overdosed. She ran to the hospital and found him in a stupor. He recovered quickly but went on to several repeat performances. Undaunted yet today, he continues to mix prescription drugs with alcohol. "I have to do this," he retorts. "It's either this or kill myself." On a typical day he struggles with PTSD until noon, at which time he rewards himself for "making it." That's when he starts consuming beer and pills. He continues until early evening, when he trails off to bed for a couple hours of sleep. At dawn, the battles and addictions start all over again.

Sarah lives each day as if it could be her husband's last. She never knows what to expect when she comes home from work. Her only hope is that if Bill does overdose, he dies peacefully.

Sarah's reaction is matter-of-fact, but realistic for many loved ones of vets unable to shake the grip of war. Spouses and other family members worry constantly that they will lose their vet to the sadness of those memories. Addictions are at least one way for the vet to find eternal peace. Substance abuse and other addictions present a terrible dilemma to loved ones. On the one hand, they say, is the disapproving look of society; on the other hand, is the vet's need to find peace and comfort.

The wife of one combat vet, in fact, actually encourages her husband to take medications to sleep and feel better. "I told him, 'either you get some medicine, or I will.'" She figures the toll of his sleeplessness (on both of them) is greater than the risk of medications.

Nancy, like many spouses of combat vets with PTSD, has reversed her opinion about medications. For years, she painfully observed her husband's battles with the memories of Vietnam. Once an adamant foe of prescribed medication, Nancy now believes it is the only way for her husband to hang on.

She is practical in her beliefs. "You wouldn't withhold drugs from a cancer patient, would you?" she asks plainly. "Keeping these guys medicated and comfortable is a must."

CHAPTER TEN

MAIMED, WOUNDED AND IN SICK BAY

PTSD AND PHYSICAL PROBLEMS

Dear Journal,
The spots came back; they're all over his back and chest. He doesn't seem very concerned, but I am. Wonder where he got 'em from. Why do they show up sometimes? Wonder if they're catching.

He complained of stomach pain again. Must be an ulcer or hope it's not stomach cancer. That would be awful. Don't know what I'd do if the doctors told me he was going to die.

He looks old now. Gray hair, tired eyes, bumps all over his body. Doesn't look well. At least he's got his legs; some of his friends don't.

I don't think he's very healthy. Looks a lot older than he is.

Me (worried to death)

MY ROTTING, DYING BODY

Maureen is still perplexed by the illness that crippled her husband, a twice-injured Vietnam combat vet. She is perplexed by the series of events leading up to his life in a wheelchair.

Maureen married Dale in 1969. Almost immediately, the physical problems began. Complaining of back and shoulder pain, Dale began a round of trips to the doctors. Finally, he ended up at a medical clinic that offered this conclusion: "It's all in your head."

But the pain lingered. Dale went to the VA Hospital, where he showed some progress under the care of a young doctor. When the young doctor left his position at the VA, Dale was unable to find another he felt as comfortable with.

Dale went back to the private health care facility and checked into the pain clinic. After a short stay, however, he suddenly left the clinic and hitched a ride home. Eventually, he put himself in a wheelchair, bunkered up in his house and never worked again. Of his baffling medical condition, Dale says, "I'm getting worse every day."

Maureen's initial shock turned to frustration and puzzlement. She eventually divorced Dale, but maintains a cordial relationship with him yet today. In spite of living apart, Maureen care-takes for her husband, even paying his house payments. She coordinates the few contacts he has with the outside world, including his doctor appointments, which he hates making. In addition to his physical condition, Dale's PTSD symptoms and behaviors have come and gone throughout the years.

Initially vacillating between anger and sadness, Maureen's feelings have settled on just being perplexed. "Why couldn't the doctors find anything wrong?" she wonders. "Is it really all in his head, or did he pick something up in 'Nam?" Her questions remain unanswered.

Dale's perplexing medical condition is not uncommon for combat vets of all generations. For centuries, warriors have returned home with all sorts of wounds, ailments and missing limbs. For centuries, loved ones have welcomed home their mangled heroes.

Some conditions wrought by war last a lifetime, and some disappear with the years. Some are recognizable, and some pose real medical mysteries.

"I JUST DON'T FEEL WELL"

When Bill returned home from Vietnam in '71, he brought back a few mementos: an expensive record player, a couple of photo albums, a bad case of PTSD (which didn't surface until 1986) and some bodily changes – deep cuts from the elephant grass, loss of pigmentation and spots that would come and go.

"I didn't really notice anything different," Bill explains of his feelings upon returning home. "I felt just fine, like any other 19-year-old." It wasn't until nearly 20 years later that Bill noticed an overall condition of not feeling well. At the same time, he unexpectedly received two Agent Orange compensation checks from a class action suit. He cashed the checks, not knowing exactly what the compensation was for or what to expect in the future.

The money didn't help Bill's feelings of not being well. Though unable to pinpoint a physical problem, Bill insists that there is one:

There's something eating away at my body. It's eating my guts, from the inside out. I know I'm dying.

So certain is Bill that he's dying, in fact, that he has bought and paid for his burial plot, located in a special veterans' area of a private cemetery. He has given his wife extensive funeral instructions and frequently queries her on the arrangements, just to make sure she remembers all the special military touches he would like. (As double insurance, Bill has also given the same set of instructions directly to the funeral home, in case his wife "screws things up.") He has even gone so far as to demand that his name be etched in the cemetery's granite memorial saved for the war-dead. "I want to see it on the memorial now, while I'm alive, so I can enjoy it." Cemetery officials have obliged Bill's quirky request. He often shows up at his plot, just "to check on it" and gaze pensively at his name on the wall. Bill's wife reacts with a mixture of fear, sadness, anger and confusion. "I want to be supportive, of course," she says. "But it's all a little too weird for me."

Bill's obsession with death results not only from his own feelings of doom but from his observations of other vet friends. "They're dying all around me," he claims. "Most of my buddies are dead now. If the war didn't get them, cancer or heart failure has." Indeed, many of Bill's vet friends have died during the past couple of years. His best bud died of a massive heart attack at age 48. Another pal died of a broken neck at age 45. And yet another friend died recently from leukemia. "They're all in their forties," Bill muses. "How come none of us makes it to 50?"

Bill's circle of friends is not unusual, it seems, in the world of combat vets, particularly those exposed to front-line action or those who served in exotic, faraway places. World War I vets endured massive trench shellings, leaving thousands upon thousands of them maimed for life. Vietnam vets suffered the ravages of Agent Orange, linked to cancer and other major illnesses. Persian Gulf vets now grapple with the "mystery illness" marked by intense pain, sleeplessness, disorientation and depression. Though the government is slow to admit the physical damages of war, it is all too clear that many warriors return home physically different than when they left.

Further plaguing Bill's circle of friends and countless other combat vets is the devastating problem of PTSD. The 48-year-old friend who died of heart failure also had PTSD and Panic Disorder; he literally blew a gasket from years of unchecked blood pressure and nervous overeating. The friend who broke his neck had actually fallen down a flight of stairs; severely depressed the day of his fall, he had overdosed on pills.

PTSD and physical problems, in fact, present a vicious cycle. The common behaviors and symptoms of PTSD – e.g., hypervigilance, recklessness, depression, substance abuse – eventually lead to physical problems. The added burden of physical problems only intensifies the PTSD.

Experts confirm that the presence of PTSD does indeed cause physiological reactions. Though still under study, the reactions have been clinically observed and documented. PTSD expert and author Dr. Aphrodite Matsakis writes about the biochemistry of PTSD in her book, *I Can't Get Over It, A Handbook for Trauma Survivors* (New Harbinger Publications, 1992):[1]

> *Like the rest of the body, your central nervous system is vulnerable. Given enough physical or emotional stress it too can bend or even break. When you experienced your trauma, your central nervous system received a series of shocks. The greater the intensity and the longer the duration of the trauma, the greater the possibility that the delicate biochemical balances of your body might have been disrupted.*

Dr. Matsakis cautions that not all trauma victims will have changed biochemistry. But for those who do, the following may be true:[2]

> *If, in fact, your biochemistry was altered by the trauma, you will likely have experienced certain problems. These problems include difficulties in thinking clearly, in regulating your emotions, in relating to other people, and, critically important, in sustaining hope for the future. Trauma-induced biological changes can also lead to or contribute to the development of clinical depression and/or a substance-abuse problem.*

Dr. Matsakis further explains the link between some trauma-induced biological changes and memory tracts in the brain. This link means that trauma victims, when reminded of the trauma, can either re-experience it or can try to numb out and avoid. "The result of these biological changes and their side effects is that the trauma is kept alive in your body, mind, and emotions."[3] She also writes of the problems associated with adrenaline surges, which occur during life-threatening situations and which contribute to the many symptoms and behaviors of PTSD.

Besides war-induced physical problems, combat vets also face the normal physical problems of their generations. World War II vets are now squaring off against the ravages of old age including cancers, heart disease, diabetes, Alzheimer's and a myriad of other life-threatening illnesses. Korean and Vietnam vets are now entering or are well into their middle years, bringing both serious problems and annoyances like bifocals and minor aches and pains.

And then there's that feeling of not being well. Many combat vets complain of having overall feelings of being sick or dying, even when there's no medical proof for such conditions. However, they pose the question: "Why would it be so unthinkable that a 45-year-old would die of cancer or heart failure? My buddy was blown to bits by a mine, and he was only 18 years old." Like Bill, who made his own funeral arrangements in his thirties, vets are not surprised when they or their friends develop illnesses and ailments far advanced for their years. They view life and death with the same matter-of-factness.

Physical ailments – war-induced, imaginary or natural progressions of age – heap more problems onto the vet with PTSD. What is often the hardest is sorting out the real pain from the PTSD pain. So strong is the connection among mind, body and soul ...

PHYSICAL PROBLEMS AND THE FAMILY

Sarah couldn't believe that she had to deal with one more of her husband's problems. Besides the frustrations surrounding Bill's PTSD and his supposed bout with Agent Orange, there have been all those minor physical things.

Last year, it was the emergency appendicitis attack and the crazy symptoms: The nose that swelled for no reason, the little bumps that appeared between his fingers and the rashes that came and vanished. "Why is it that no one else has these weird diseases?" she asks. Sarah is certain that Bill's only problem is a severe case of hypochondria.

When Bill first complained of stomach pain, Sarah ignored him. When he complained a little louder, she bought him a couple bottles of liquid stuff to drink. When he continued to complain, she finally brought him to the clinic, convinced that doctors there would pooh-pooh the whole thing.

The doctors did brush Bill away, saying that he had gas pains resulting from a poor diet. Bill was persistent, though, and asked to be taken back to the clinic. Sarah reluctantly scheduled another appointment. For a second time, the doctors said Bill was just fine. He did not have any serious medical condition, they concluded. Sarah was relieved; she felt certain her husband's hypochondria would settle down for a while. But she was wrong. Bill insisted that he be taken back yet a third time to the clinic. Sarah was furious; each doctor visit cost money and time away from her job (Bill doesn't drive).

But she was forced to oblige. Bill went back to the clinic a third time, and finally found a doctor who agreed with him. Bill was indeed suffering from something real, probably ulcers or stomach cancer. Bill went through a battery of tests, which uncovered a diseased gall bladder. He went in for same-day surgery, and then home to recuperate.

Sarah was relieved. Whew! Now that Bill's problem had been found and solved, he should be on his way to recovery. And she should be able to move on with her life and her job. Back to normal.

During Bill's recovery at home, a massive snowstorm hit the area. Sarah warned Bill to stay in bed, per the doctor's instructions. She would shovel the snow, she advised, or would hire the neighborhood kids to do it. But Bill wouldn't hear of it. He leapt out of his sickbed, threw his clothes on and ran outside to face the knee-high drifts of snow. Not only did he shovel his own driveway, but he did the neighbor's as well.

Bill became extremely sick. He crawled back into bed, where he stayed for several days. His temperature climbed steadily, and his stomach pains intensified. The area surrounding the wound changed colors, from blue to yellow to red to blue again. Sarah concluded that Bill was hemorrhaging. Back to the doctor, and more time off from work.

The doctor verified that Bill was indeed bleeding. He would have to go back to surgery. So off they went, back to the hospital. Bill's wound was cleaned, and he was released the same afternoon. Sarah took her husband home to bed. She sighed in relief, and went to bed early herself. Maybe now the problem was over. Back to normal.

Bill became depressed and began drinking within 24 hours of the second surgery. He became intoxicated and verbally abusive. He began throwing things around the house, including a glass cup. Sarah wrestled with Bill to get the glass from him; the two tangled for a while, further agitating the injury. Bill finally succumbed to the pain and laid down to sleep. For the next couple of weeks, he kept a low profile, and eventually recovered. But Sarah remained exhausted, furious and depressed for quite a while:

Having to deal with Bill's PTSD is bad enough. He's often drunk and abusive. But add to it any physical problem, and things get way out of hand. Bill gets ornery when he doesn't feel well, and he takes it out on me because I'm the one who's there. I get sick and tired, too, of his impulsiveness; he does so many dumb things that hurt himself and me. I wish he'd grow up and use some sense – if he has any.

Sarah expresses the sentiments of many loved ones of vets with the dual problem of PTSD and physical ailments. Their plate is too full, they say; the vet's needs are just too intense and too overwhelming. Because he cannot make decisions or handle day-to-day tasks of living, they are forced to fill in – again. They make the doctor appointments, handle the insurance papers, pick up the prescriptions, call employers about absences, etc. They also take on the job of explaining the vet's physical problems to outsiders, including the skeptical. While most loved ones say it is far harder to explain PTSD to others, all agree it is nearly impossible to explain the presence of both PTSD and physical problems.

For loved ones of vets who are middle age, the problems of older parents may put them in a real squeeze-play for time and attention. And physical problems are never cheap; the financial toll can be horrendous.

Care-takers themselves become fatigued, resentful or ill. They go bankrupt, from the inside out.

Sarah tells of being unable to find the time for her own health needs. She has missed many doctor appointments; for one entire year, she has ignored her doctor's orders to have a full blood profile done for both thyroid and cholesterol checks. Ashamed to enter the doctor's office, Sarah also missed her annual mammogram, despite a family history of breast cancer. "I know, I know – I'll get to it," she claims. But Sarah's work schedule and husband's minute-by-minute demands make it unlikely she will fit in a doctor appointment any time soon.

Like the vet with PTSD, loved ones also complain of physical problems related to having secondary PTSD. Living with the disorder and all its stresses and uncertainties often leads to problems similar to those of the vet. The problems are real and even life-threatening.

During her marriage to a Vietnam combat vet, Cindy had constant chest pains, made better only by a personal wellness plan of exercise and a healthy diet. When her marriage to a combat vet becomes especially stressful, Sandra is treated for high blood pressure. And years of living with her World War II vet, have given Mabel a nervous condition similar to that of her husband.

Sometimes loved ones of vets with PTSD get physical scars at the hands of their vet. Violence and domestic abuse are a frequent by-product of the disorder and a frequent presence in the home. Serious injuries often result, as do trips to the emergency room. Living with PTSD can be very dangerous to one's health.

Barry is the son of a combat vet with uncontrollable anger. As a child, Barry contracted an illness and missed an entire year of school. While the illness took a terrible toll on the boy's health and psyche, far worse was the treatment he received from his father. A commanding man with a large physical presence, his father taunted and beat him, worsening his physical state and throwing him into depression. Though five years in the past, the scars of abuse still affect Barry's physical and emotional health.

Like the aging vet, loved ones suffer from physical ailments natural to their ages and unrelated to PTSD. As in any family, children of vets get the mumps and the measles and strep throat. They fall off their bikes and get all the scratches and scrapes natural to growing up. Spouses, too, wear the ravages of the middle and golden years; they get the same illnesses, wrinkles and dark circles as any one else their age. But the vicissitudes of life are magnified by the presence of PTSD.

Barbara has severe back problems, like others in their early forties. She has been in and out of surgery for years. Today, she can barely sit without pursing her lips; the pain is always there.

Though now divorced from her husband, a Vietnam combat vet, Barbara tells of enduring fierce pain while facing the everyday problems of PTSD. The worst incident, she remembers, was when her son ran away to escape the abuses of his stepdad (her husband). The boy stole a car and drove more than a thousand miles away. Only two weeks from having back surgery, Barbara went to fetch her son. "My back was already killing me, but the drive down there was really bad," she sighs. During her 10-year marriage, Barbara's back paid a big price. The pain never went away.

Families of combat vets also live with the extreme physical problems wrought by war itself – the carnage of bombs, shellings and chemical attacks. For the spouse of a vet without limbs, the responsibilities are mind-boggling.

For families whose children are born with birth defects from Agent Orange or the Gulf War mystery illness, the responsibilities last a lifetime.

And sometimes severe physical problems are created by the sheer lunacy of PTSD, the recklessness of the adrenaline rush. Nancy's husband was shot five times in the stomach during an assortment of barroom brawls. Other family members tell of their vet's car wrecks, wild sporting events, fist fights and on-the-job injuries. Again, the carnage is terrible; families deal not only with PTSD, but with broken bones, limbs and even death.

Among the hardest thing to deal with, however, is the vet's feelings of imminent death. Loved ones are confused by these feelings; they don't know whether they portend real things to come, or if they are just another symptom of PTSD. They tire of the endless instructions to "get the papers in order," "make sure you get the honor guard for my funeral" and "it's a good thing you have a job, because I won't be around much longer." Like Sarah, who doubted her husband's physical problems, many loved ones think such statements are the ramblings of a tired, old soldier.

But death is a reality for many combat vets. They return from war maimed, wounded and ill; or they become maimed, wounded or ill from years of untreated PTSD. Often, their own feelings of death and dying contribute to their overall lack of well-being. They have seen death at a young age, and they watch their buddies die off far before their time.

For loved ones on the sidelines, those feelings of mortality are hard to deal with. How do you assure your vet that he will live, even though he never feels well? How do you comfort your vet at the funeral of his best buddy? How do you plan for life without him?

Besides the devastation of physical problems, imagined or not, depression plays a major role in the mortality of combat vets. Depression is discussed at length in the next chapter.

CHAPTER ELEVEN

EMOTIONALLY AWOL:
I CAN'T MAKE IT ONE MORE DAY

PTSD AND DEPRESSION

Dear Journal,
He's so sad all the time. His big frame gets so hunched over when he cries. Some days, that's all he does. Cries and cries. Don't know why he cries so much. Maybe it's for all the guys he lost over there.
Wonder if he'd ever kill himself. Seems like he gets sad enough to. He's got guns all over the house. Wouldn't be surprised to come home some day and find him dead. Brains all over the wall. That'd be unbearable. Hope the kids don't see it if it does happen.
Hard for me to know what to say, what to do when he's so down. There's like this little cloud following him around all day. Guess all I can do is be there for him. Makes all of us sad, too.

Me (praying he doesn't kill himself)

THE LIVING DEAD

When the wife of one combat vet describes her husband, she recalls the black-and-white science fiction movie, the one with the legion of dead soldiers marching, marching through a field of mist. "My husband's like that," she says quietly. "He reminds me of one of those old Civil War soldiers in that movie." Moving slowly, lifelessly across an empty plain, towards an empty future.

Many families describe their vets with PTSD as the "living dead," elusive and hard to hang on to. They say, even though his body made it home, his heart and his soul did not. They speak of the "other woman" – Vietnam, Korea, the South Pacific – and of the faraway, hollow look of the eyes. They know, all too well, that their vet may succumb to the pain of the past. They know he may slip through their lives into eternal peace.

DEPRESSION AND SUICIDE

Depression goes hand-in-hand with many of the other symptoms and behaviors of PTSD. It is often associated with panic, feelings of helplessness, grief, survival guilt, substance abuse and anger. Clinicians speak of normal feelings of grief following a real loss, such as death of a loved one. And then they refer to clinical depression, the kind that many vets with PTSD have and the kind that worsens with time. Many experts believe that Vietnam vets in particular have been depressed since the war. But even vets of World War II, a publicly supported war, battle depression while trying to enjoy retirement.

There are many causes of clinical depression. Readers are advised to consult Dr. Aphrodite Matsakis' book, *I Can't Get Over It, A Handbook for Trauma Survivors* (New Harbinger Publications, 1992) or another such source for an in-depth discussion of those causes. Suffice it to say that trauma victims are an easy target for clinical depression.

Unlike normal grief feelings, clinical depression is usually linked with "grief over psychological or spiritual loss, such as a loss of innocence, a loss of a belief once held dear, or the loss of self-respect" (Matsakis, *I Can't Get Over It, A Handbook for Trauma Survivors*).[1] PTSD is also viewed as a spiritual problem; after all, how can the returning warrior have feelings of God and goodness intact, when he has just committed the most unspeakable of acts?

In her book, *Recovering from the War* (Penguin Books, 1990), Patience Mason aptly sums up the vet's overwhelming feelings of grief; though the reference is to Vietnam, certainly vets of other wars suffer losses as well:[2]

Veterans lost more than people in Vietnam. Grief can also be for lost ideals, for lost belief in leaders, for loss of the innate knowledge that nothing really bad can happen, for learning that one is expendable, for one's self-respect, for that other life each guy lost in Vietnam. Some lost their futures. Some lost hope. Some lost the ability to love or trust or care for anyone.

The wife of one combat vet describes the kinds of questions the two of them wrestle with nearly every day. "Recently, he was watching some kind of emotional TV show. I think one of the main characters died or something. My husband turned to me, tears in his eyes, and said, 'Am I going to heaven?' I don't know what makes him think he won't, except for Vietnam."

According to the U.S. Department of Health and Human Services, the symptoms of depression are as follows: Persistent sadness or feelings of emptiness; a sense of hopelessness; feelings of guilt; problems sleeping; loss of interest or pleasure in ordinary activities; fatigue or decreased energy; and difficulty concentrating, remembering, and making decisions.[3]

Loved ones of vets with PTSD describe the difficulties and sadness of living with depression. They also express difficulty in keeping their own spirits up. It's not easy being a cheerleader.

THE TIRED CHEERLEADER

For years, Nancy propped up her husband's self-esteem. She was his one-woman cheering section, helping him seek treatment for depression and spending hours each day trying to ease his loneliness and feelings of unworthiness.

But through the years, the cheering has come harder for Nancy. She's tired. And she's not totally convinced that life is the better alternative for her husband. "Sometimes I think he would be better off dead," she explains. Only then would he find peace.

Fatigue, frustration, hopelessness and helplessness are common in families of vets battling PTSD. Loved ones complain of feeling dragged down by their vet's depression. Life no longer holds great promise for them either. They also complain of sugar-coating things to avoid upsetting the vet; they run around with a false smile and a false aura of elation. Psychotherapist Kathryn Berg describes the futility of trying to cheer someone up: "Sometimes the family will go through their dance to cheer the person up or bounce them out of it, which is usually ineffective."[4]

At its simplest, depression interferes with the normal routine of living and working and breathing. "The veteran is not a fully, active, participating member of the family when it comes to work, chores or recreation activities," explains Dr. Arthur Blank, Jr., psychiatrist and PTSD expert.[5] For those around him, the vet's dropping-out means a loss of help, warmth and companionship.

It also means confusion and resentment on the part of family members, who almost always have to pick up the pieces, filling in for the vet's lack of interest or energy. To family members, psychotherapist Kathryn Berg explains, depression looks like a complete "shutdown".[6]

At the extreme, depression can be a life-threatening presence in the home. Talk of death and thoughts of suicide are constant reminders of the vet's pain and unresolved past. Spouses and children speak of guns under the pillow and sleeping pills at hand. They shudder at the vet's pronouncements: "You'd be better off without me ... I shouldn't have made it back from the war ... I died 20 years ago ... The only time I'll be happy is when they plant me."

Though data surrounding the studies are controversial, there are plenty of professionals who feel that Vietnam veterans have higher-than-average suicide risks. If this is true, then the fears of family members are realistic indeed.

So intense is the fear of suicide, in fact, that many loved ones plan their lives around the vet's whims and feelings. Many spouses are afraid to leave their vet alone, even for an hour or two; they rush through errands like there's a fire at home. One spouse says she so fears her husband's whimsical depression that she would not be surprised to walk into her home to find his brains splattered all over the wall. She cringes at the sight of a police car or ambulance. "It's probably going to my house!" she says. Like others who live around PTSD, she, too, has intrusive thoughts and panic attacks. She experiences sudden moments of terror in public, imagining the worst is happening at home.

For many spouses and children, the "no-hope syndrome" is more than they can handle. Their vet's feelings of hopelessness, and sometimes their own, often leads to extreme symptoms and behaviors on their part. Some opt to remove themselves from the depression by leaving the marriage or running away from home. And others find themselves slipping into a sea of depression. "As research has shown," writes Dr. Aphrodite Matsakis, "suicide in the family is a significant risk factor for suicide in the other family members" (*Vietnam Wives*, Woodbine House, 1988).[7] When family members find themselves flirting with the idea of suicide, they should certainly seek professional help.

Barbara describes the cycle of pain and depression in her marriage. Her vet husband's PTSD and depression not only impacted her, but the couple's children as well:

Oh God, it's just mind-numbing to think about it ... I was on medication by the end of the summer. I was very depressed and had gone to my clinic and talked to them. We were all in so much pain, I don't think anything could have helped. I wish I would have left before we ever got to that point.

The couple split, and Barbara got better through the years. But depression continues to haunt the couple's son.

Mark (deceased) was a Vietnam combat vet whose PTSD and depression marred every aspect of his family's life. While alive, his wife and three young sons battled the demons of depression right alongside him. Upon his death, all four survivors plummeted into deep depression. Most affected were his two oldest sons, both of whom attempted suicide; the sons have been diagnosed with severe cases of PTSD themselves. And Mark's wife took up a variety of reckless habits after his death. Depression, both before and after Mark's death, seemed to overtake the household.

THE SEASON OF MOURNING

To every thing there is a season, and a time to every purpose under the heaven:

A time to be born, and a time to die; a time to plant, and a time to pluck up that which is planted;

A time to kill, and a time to heal; a time to break down, and a time to build up;

A time to weep, and a time to laugh; a time to mourn, and a time to dance;

A time to cast away stones, and a time to gather stones together; a time to embrace, and a time to refrain from embracing;

A time to get, and a time to lose; a time to keep, and a time to cast away;

A time to rend, and a time to sew; a time to keep silence, and a time to speak;

A time to love, and a time to hate; a time of war, and a time of peace.
                                                    – Ecclesiastes, Chapter 3, Verses 1-8

After the big guns quit and the soldiers go home, the natural "season of mourning" begins. Soldiers have many things to mourn – the loss of friends in battle and the loss of their youth and innocence on the battlefield. As they cry, they hopefully begin the season of healing and the season of starting a new life.

But often, as with PTSD, the season of mourning never takes place at all, or it takes place years after war. Sometimes the mourning never stops, and the healing never begins. Sometimes there's an eternal hole in the heart:

I will never get over war. I will never forget those friends I lost. They were like family to me. I don't care if it's 30 years later. I still cry for them, and I don't feel any better.
* – Bill, Vietnam combat vet*

Sometimes the soldier in mourning carries his grief from the actual battlefield to the home battlefield. Families frequently come face-to-face with their vet's season of mourning. It can mystify, confuse and frighten them; often, the source of the pain is unclear. From whence the sadness and tears come, they do not know. What they do know is that their loved one hurts, and he hurts with a depth they have never seen.

When Cheryl's husband lost his father, he cried with an intensity she had not expected. He cried and cried for days, she says, totally unable to contain his grief. Cheryl decided the source of her husband's pain was far broader than this single death. "You're crying for all those guys in Vietnam, too," she told him.

Tracy has had a hard time sorting out her husband's hot-cold emotions about death. She is mystified by his refusal to attend his own father's funeral a couple of years ago. The funeral took place in another state; Richard, her husband, simply stated that it was too far to drive. He never paid his last respects, and he never cried.

And yet, at the death of a fellow vet friend whom he had known for only a few years, Richard fell apart. This is the first time Tracy recalls seeing him cry over the death of anyone. Scared by his own reaction, Richard asked, "Why am I crying? Why do I feel this so much?" He hadn't even reacted that strongly to the death of his friend, Sam, who died alongside him in 'Nam. Sam had died walking point for Richard while Richard stopped for a smoke. Sam went on ahead another 100 yards and was shot.

Tracy thinks she knows the reason for Richard's reactions to the more recent death:

I think that maybe he was finally starting to deal with the whole thing. I think part of his friend was his dad. When they were over there (Vietnam), they shut everything off. Yah, we lost Sam today, but you shut the door and start the next day. But here at home 25-30 years later, that door's not there to shut. Over there in combat, there was somebody to take Sam's place right there. Here in the real world, there's nobody there the next day.

Tracy thinks Richard's streams and streams of tears are for his dad and all the people he has lost, both in Vietnam and since. Though delayed, the season of mourning has finally begun. And Tracy, like millions of other family members, is there to help her vet get through it.

She also hopes to be there for the next season. The season of healing.

CHAPTER TWELVE

ON LEAVE AND IN PORT ...

PTSD AND MONEY PROBLEMS

Dear Journal,
 Damn, I get so tired of being broke! We never seem to make it to the end of the month. His disability checks just don't go far enough. Would be lucky to come up with five cents.
 I'd like to work, but he doesn't want me to. Wants me to be here all the time with him. Says it makes him feel better.
 Guess we'll just have to learn how to make ends meet. Wonder where I could cut back. Would be nice to save a little, but there's just no way ...

 Me (broke again!)

BROKE, AGAIN

Al and Mary figure if they pool their loose change, they can buy enough gas to get home from their friend's house. They've had a lovely, carefree weekend. But now they've got to face facts: Once again, they're dead broke.

But hey, man, it's the end of the month. What do you expect? Al's government disability checks for PTSD don't go very far, especially if you own a home and like to smoke pot. Especially if neither of you works and has no other source of income. Man, it's a long, long month.

Al and Mary, like countless other families living and coping with PTSD, find that money (or the lack thereof) is a constant issue in their lives. The topic of "money" crops up all the time – a constant in any decision and an undercurrent in all households with PTSD.

AT ODDS WITH MAKING A LIVING

Soldiers and sailors have long suffered an image problem with money. "Like a drunken sailor on leave" is a common expression for throwing money around. Movies popularly portray soldiers playing craps and betting their meager pay in the process. The happy-go-lucky serviceman loses his shirt, but knows his next meal will come, courtesy of Uncle Sam.

But in civilian life, the next meal is not so certain. While most veterans leave the service to lead productive lives, a percentage do not. For them, the symptoms and behaviors of PTSD make it difficult to make a living. Their problems are at great odds with successful employment:

- Relationship problems – *I can't stand my co-workers; they bug me or they're always picking on me. Wish I could work alone.*
- Alienation – *I hate my job. It's boring. I'm not very interested in my work.*
- Anger/Rage – *I'd like to pop so-and-so in the nose! He makes me so mad I could shoot him!*
- Helplessness – *I feel so insignificant at work. I'm not important here. I'm stuck in a rut until the day I die.*
- Anxiety/Panic – *I'm so hyper, I just can't sit at that desk all day. My heart is racing a thousand miles a minute. I feel like I'm having a heart attack, right here in the office!*
- Sleep Disturbance – *I'm so tired at work, I could fall asleep at my machine. Wish I could get some sleep at night.*
- Startle Reaction – *When my truck backfires, I hit the deck! I wish you wouldn't sneak up at my desk like that.*
- Memory Problems – *No, I don't remember what we discussed at the meeting yesterday. Could you refresh me?*
- Distrust of Authority – *I hate my boss! I just know he's out to get me.*
- Substance Abuse – *I'm having a hard time operating my press; I'm high by the time I get to work in the morning.*

Any combination of these symptoms and behaviors makes for a very problematic employee and lots of unemployment. According to author and Vietnam vet Chuck Dean, one out of four Vietnam combat vets makes less than $7,000 a year (excerpted from the book *Making Peace with Your Past: Nam Vet*, by Chuck Dean, Multnomah Books, Questar Publishers, copyright

1988 by Chuck Dean).[1] Lower yet on the economic scale are homeless vets, who blight every major American city across the country. Data shows that one in three homeless persons is a veteran, with as many as 230,000-250,000 on the street during any given night. According to statistics compiled by the American Legion, homeless vets break down as follows: 10 percent served in World War II, 13.4 percent in Korea, 51.7 percent in Vietnam and the rest during other eras including peacetime.[2]

PTSD is hard on the pocketbook.

FAMILIES AND MONEY WOES

Spouses often mirror their vet's problems, so for them making a living is also a challenge. The effects of secondary PTSD wear hard on those who live around the vet. They, too, often become unemployable.

For Mary, the challenge is her own bad back, which keeps her from working, and her husband's relentless demands. Though tired of being broke, Mary has to be within earshot of Al, who has PTSD and panic attacks. He gets nervous when she's not right there. In a crowd, he needs her to sit next to him, knees touching. Despite their desperate need for cash, Al can't let Mary go off to work and leave him alone; he simply can't make it through the day without her.

Patty, though a self-described gypsy who doesn't mind following her husband's wanderlust, owns very few materials things. She does without perfumes and new furniture. Now in her early fifties, she is used to completely starting over. Patty gave up her professional business career to stay at home and meet her husband's minute-by-minute demands. There's absolutely no time in her schedule for a job, she claims. "I don't know how a woman could possibly handle PTSD and even kids, too." Once a dynamic, social woman, Patty has developed some of the same PTSD symptoms and behaviors as her husband; she dreads being around people and suffers from depression.

Patty and her husband once tried going into business for themselves. For a while, dog-breeding was very rewarding. They could run their business at home, set their own pace and be their own boss. But soon, Patty's husband resented the pressures of having to be there all the time; he likes to disappear for a few days, no strings attached. The couple gave up the business, and now subsist on Al's government checks for PTSD. Patty, like others dependent on assistance, panics when the mail is late or some mix-up happens. Her life is tied to the mailbox.

Doing without is commonplace for families with PTSD. Those who do not receive compensation checks at all and whose members are unemployed face the harshest problems yet. These are families living on the edge. Besides having no income, they have none of the fringe benefits of health care, property and long-term savings plans. These are America's poorest.

Since divorcing, Barbara's world is far different than the one she shared with her Vietnam vet husband. She relishes in her escape from PTSD; she enjoys being away from her husband's violence, drug abuse and depression. Still, the money worries cut deep. She has physical problems that keep her from working; she and her two children live on small government checks. Though her husband now receives PTSD payments, he shares none of his income with them.

Barbara's world is stark. She and her children live in a basement apartment with three tiny rooms. They share a bathroom with several other families; they have to walk across the hall to shower or use the toilet. There's no toilet paper, and the towels haven't been washed in a long time. Soiled clothes cover the bathroom floor, and there's a strong smell of urine.

For spouses who do work, the pressures are often as great or more so. If they are the sole supporters of their families, they live with the stress of bringing in the only paycheck. Their employment also brings health coverage and other needed benefits to the family. For them, life is a series of lonely battles; they face not only the horrors of PTSD, but they also balance the checkbook, ward off the creditors and even parent the kids alone. They juggle work with PTA meetings. And they throw in a load of clothes between making dinner and helping Sally with homework. Though there's a paycheck, the family's welfare is still in jeopardy because the spouse's health is always at risk.

Sarah shares the pressures of being an employed professional living with a husband who has rampant PTSD. Her job requires constant attention to details and deadlines; she is often called upon to work weekends and evenings. "All the while I'm at work," she explains, "I worry what Bill is up to. Will he have a flashback while I'm at my meeting? Will he make good on his threat to shoot up the neighborhood?" Though Sarah enjoys the income and financial freedom her job affords, she is certain the pressures are not worth it. She daydreams about quitting and settling in to a simpler lifestyle.

Tracy, wife of a Vietnam combat vet, is pleased that her husband has worked seven years on one job. "It's a record!" she exclaims. Throughout their married life, her husband has jumped from job to job:

> *He'd work for six months and then, "I can't do it anymore." His problem is just the getting up and going to work; he just did not want to face anyone, face the world I guess.*
>
> *Things would start going good, he gets a new job and he's all excited, so we start making some plans. That's gone. I guess I figured I was going to be working all of my adult life anyway. So it's not as if I felt he pushed me out of the home to go to work cuz you know, I was working when I met him, worked before and I've worked ever since.*

Tracy complains little about working full-time and caring entirely for the home and kids. The family lives in a modest townhome with modest furnishings. For Tracy, there are no trips, no shopping sprees, no new clothes in the family budget.

Spouses are not the only ones affected financially by the vet's PTSD. Children, too, often mirror their parents' financial woes.

Kevin and Shannon are typical children of Vietnam combat vets. Both in their early to mid-twenties, their lives until now have been tangled webs of substance abuse, dropping out of school and encounters with the law. Though trying to settle down, both are late comers to the employment scene. Neither has job prospects or hopes of moving out of their parents' homes. For each, self-sufficiency is but a dream.

For combat vets who live with their parents, the future is especially precarious. Ron and Doris wonder what will become of their son, a Vietnam vet with PTSD, when they die. Already well into their senior years, they know their son will have a hard time making it on his own. Their son gets compensation checks, but it is they who actually care for him; they provide him room and board and, most importantly, companionship and understanding. No amount of money will make up for that when they are gone.

Shirley, too, endures the worry of a parent. She worries that her son, Tom, and his own young son, both of whom live with her on a small farm in the Midwest, will not make it when she's gone. Well into her senior years, Shirley is realistic in her assessment of Tom's abilities to handle life. She also worries about their economic security. Tom receives no compensation for PTSD and is not likely to pursue it because he hates red tape and filling out forms. His only income is welfare checks for his son, which Shirley accepts with mixed feelings:

He's gettin' welfare for the boy, so that gives him a little outlet. That gives him spending money and that helps out and he gets food stamps. No way would I ever take food stamps. When Tom's father died, we had an old car that needed a heater. Everybody at work told me to go down to welfare to see if I could get help. They said, "no, we can't help you. We'll give you food stamps." I refused. I'll get my car fixed. You know, I got that stupid, dumb pride. I don't want any food stamps and I don't like him being on welfare, but I accept it and life goes on.

UNHEALTHY ATTITUDE TOWARDS MONEY

Besides not having enough of it, families with PTSD battle mixed feelings about money and economic well-being. They see their security slip through the vet's fingers with his impulsive and reactive lifestyle. They suffer his wild nights on the town and quick purchases that mask futile attempts to run from the memories of war. They see his free spending deplete the family resources. They panic about tomorrow. They dread the arrival of the monthly bank statement.

But sometimes families of vets with PTSD suffer a far different kind of money problem. Sometimes they live with the workaholic vet, who toils nonstop to forget his bad memories, or the miserly vet, who stockpiles money to make himself happy. Families in homes like these suffer, too; though their security is not threatened, their daily comforts can be meager.

Cindy remembers living with her workaholic husband. He worked three jobs, and saved it all. He had bank accounts and property all over town. Though now divorced, the couple remembers those days differently. Cindy's husband remembers those working days as happy ones. "I was worth nearly a million dollars," he brags. But Cindy doesn't share fond memories of those times. She remembers her husband rarely stopping to be with her and their young daughter. She worked right alongside him just to spend some time together.

Cindy now knows her husband worked like that to avoid dealing with Vietnam. When the memories eventually overtook him, he crashed. But he never changed his view of money. He continued to stockpile cash and property using the various disability checks he received. He saved things in his name only, rarely sharing the money with his wife. Upon their divorce, Cindy received less than half the couple's assets. Her husband explains his behavior this way: "Security is very important to me. I had to protect myself, had to think about tomorrow. Like being back in the army. You gotta be ready at all times."

Another spouse tells of her husband's total cheapness. She has not received a gift from him in years, and he deprives her of any spending money. "It's a good thing I work," she says, "or I'd probably never eat or have clothes on my back." She also marvels at her husband's strange vacillation between extravagance and miserliness:

One day, he's talking about buying a big boat, and the next day he acts like we're headed for the soup line. I wish he would just see money for what it is; a way to enjoy life. It's not to be worshipped, and it's not to be despised.

She hates her husband's obsession with money, and how it plays such a major role in his happiness and self-respect. She believes that his vacillation is due entirely to PTSD. The occasional extravagance is a way to run from Vietnam, a devil-may-care attitude that says, "I won't be here tomorrow, anyway." She sees the miserliness as stemming from the need to be prepared, ready for the day "when the troops pull out and your sack better be packed." It's like a doomsday feeling, she says.

Whether working or spending like there's no tomorrow, or simply living from paycheck to paycheck, vets with PTSD often have a love-hate relationship with money. Realistically, they know they have to have it to survive; but the ravages of PTSD make it difficult to earn a living. The guilt of just surviving makes them wonder if they deserve a decent life.

Financial insecurities also plague those living with the vet. They suffer when there's not enough money to go around, and they suffer when there's an unhealthy attitude towards money. Whatever the circumstance, money is almost certainly a big issue in homes with PTSD. (*Author's note:* Government compensation for PTSD is further addressed in Chapter 14.)

CHAPTER THIRTEEN

WACS, WAVES AND WAR

PTSD, FEMALE VETS AND THEIR FAMILIES

Dear Journal,
   I know this friend at work who was in the Army or Navy, not sure which one. Really nice person, a lot of fun. But she doesn't get along with the guys. Told me once it has something to do with being raped in the service. Must have been terrible. She never mentioned it again. Come to think of it, she's not married or anything. Kind of keeps to herself a lot. Don't know much more about her.
   I heard stories of nurses in 'Nam who have a hard time with it. Must have seen a lot of guys dying. Heard they keep to themselves pretty much, too. Glad I never joined the service. Pretty hard on women. Like they have their own kind of war ...

   Me

A CENTURIES-OLD STORY

Media surrounded the entry of women into combat during the Persian Gulf War. The story of one woman POW drew special attention; she had not only been captured but sexually assaulted as well.

But women and war is actually an old story. For centuries, women have fought bravely alongside their male counterparts. They were a common sight on the American frontier, battling all sorts of enemies and elements. They fought (often disguised as men) in major wars, and they have always been near the battlefield, patching up the sick and saying good-bye to the mortally wounded. Women have been trainers, journalists, entertainers, support personnel, pilots and – in Desert Storm – infantry soldiers. Though not front-line, hand-to-hand combatants, women vets perform their service duties with a passion. Their jobs are important. Sometimes they're even in charge.

In Vietnam, females played a particularly significant role. It is estimated that 8-11,000 women served in Vietnam, most of them as nurses. The contributions of these female veterans is eulogized in many a poem and a prayer; a permanent tribute was erected in 1993 with the Vietnam Women's Memorial in Washington, D.C.

Like their male counterparts, women suffer from their military experiences. Experts agree that trauma is trauma; it knows no age, cultural, economic, religious or gender differences. Estimates vary as to the number of women who have PTSD. From the Vietnam War alone, it is estimated that 21 percent of the female vets have some degree of the disorder.[1] There are additional victims from the Persian Gulf, as evidenced by women's support groups springing up from that war.

However, while female vets do indeed have PTSD, the source of their PTSD often differs from male vets. And women have a tougher time convincing the "system" that they suffer and are in need of treatment and support. According to an article in *DAV Magazine*:[2]

> *The stigma of mental illness and the risk of jeopardizing a military career – many women who served in Vietnam are still on active duty – are two factors that have contributed to women with PTSD from not seeking professional help.*
>
> *Similar to male Vietnam veterans, the recent Persian Gulf War triggered memories of traumatic experiences for women Vietnam veterans, 80 percent of whom were nurses. Having served primarily as care-givers rather than as infantry troops, however, their symptoms relate more to a sense of not having done enough to save a wounded soldier rather than the survivor guilt a combat veteran may feel. Consequently, they may try to avoid or deny troubling feelings about their experiences.*

Many nurses tell of the bloodiness and lunacy of battle. So young themselves, they tell of holding young men in their arms while they die. Such a helpless feeling. "What more could I have done?" they ask, over and over through the passing years.

A second experience differentiates women vets with PTSD from their male counterparts. Sexual harassment of women in the armed forces is well-documented in national media coverage. Sexual trauma is the focus of the Women's Trauma Recovery Program at the National Center for PTSD in Menlo Park. According to Director Fred Gusman, the program is a trailblazer across the country:[3]

> *(The program) was initiated in response to women who were suffering from war zone-related stress. That would be women who served in Vietnam, Korea, the Gulf War, or as we are involved in more peace-keeping missions, there are women who are participating in those missions.*
>
> *... and then Tail Hook happened soon after we opened, and there was a request by Washington for us to expand our program to treat women who suffered sexual trauma while serving in the military.*
>
> *Our program now has shifted where it's primarily sexual trauma because there's such a demand for that focus of treatment.*

Though the source of PTSD may differ between men and women, their suffering is the same. Women vets endure the same symptoms and behaviors of the disorder. Their lives are also disrupted by service to their country. They, too, return home a lot different than when they left.

COMBAT – A STATE OF MIND

Christy is a small, five-foot tall woman with lots of energy. She recalls wanting to join the service ever since sixth grade. "I was bent on joining the Marines," she explains, "but then I saw a helicopter and changed my mind. I was hooked." After graduation, Christy joined the National Guard, and then switched to regular army. She loved her job in flight operations, and reveled in her duties with dispatch and air traffic control. Her only regret was not going to war (she had joined during peacetime). Still, she loved her job and she was darn good at it.

Then the traumas began, one right after the other for the next eight years. The first is still most painful. Christy remembers driving a tanker cross-country when she had a premonition that something was wrong at home. It was 4:30 in the morning, and she knew she had to find out. "I called, and my mom said, 'Happy birthday, you're dad's dead.'" Christy couldn't believe the accuracy of her prediction, and the flatness of the message.

She went home for the funeral. The oldest of eight, she recalls her mom and younger brothers and sisters begging her to stay, and the pain of saying no to them. In fact, Christy was glad to escape back to the army. "I could run away from it," she admits.

Two weeks later Christy had bad dreams about her father's funeral. It was 2:30 in the morning when she felt the presence of someone in the barracks. The assault didn't last long, but she remembers the feel of the fatigue shirt over her face and the scent of the man attacking her. She also remembers feeling strange, like she was floating above her body and watching her dad's funeral.

The hours following the assault were even more traumatic. Christy was grilled about her virginity (she was a virgin, evidenced by the profuse bleeding), and given an abortion pill. During the ambulance ride on the way to the hospital, she was further grilled on what she had done to prompt the attack. After the physical exam, Christy sat in a flimsy nightgown in full view of passers-by, until someone from her company came to pick her up. The assault was eventually classified a rape, but no one was ever prosecuted.

Still, Christy loved the service. She didn't regret joining. But she did wonder, over and over, how the rape could have occurred in a barracks surrounded by MP's. She also marvels at the lack of eyewitnesses.

A few months later, Christy's 41-year-old mom died of a massive heart attack. She hurried home in time to make all the arrangements. Once again, she faced the pleas of seven younger siblings, and once again, she refused to stay. "I didn't want to raise seven kids," she says. "I enjoyed playing the aunt who visited once in a while." Christy's grandparents got her off the hook. They stepped in and offered to raise the children.

A few short months later, Christy got another call from home. This time it was her grandfather; he had suffered a heart attack and died. Christy was shocked. "Every time I go home, it's for a funeral," she said. She was also painfully aware of her negligence in dealing with her brothers and sisters. Here they were, being raised by an old grandmother. Once more, Christy fled back to the army.

On a collision course with trauma, Christy next suffered a helicopter crash. It was only a few months after her last visit home. The copter she was riding lost hydraulics above the trees and rolled to the ground. Christy's seat belt malfunctioned, and she sustained injuries. Her pain lasted for the next four years, during which she was in and out of casts.

Christy describes the next episode in her military career as the happiest. Transferred to an air base abroad, she enjoyed "eventful times," as she describes it. She thrived on the constant round of dignitaries that flew in and out of the base. "We were always on alert – it was very exciting." And she loved her work.

Then it all unraveled. The nervous breakdown (over a boyfriend, she sighs); the knee replacement surgery; and the head-to-head battles with a sergeant major in charge. "He tried to force me to be a clerk," she screams. "But I was in flight ops – I wasn't going to shuffle papers."

But the sergeant major had it in for her. He stuck her in an office, which she hated. Problems escalated, and Christy was "put out of the service," as she labels it, in the mid-1980's. Her eight-year career was over, and her life's dreams were gone. "I didn't want to leave the military," she says quietly. "I felt like I was really at home there."

Throughout her military career, Christy suffered PTSD symptoms and behaviors. The nightmares, lack of emotions, volatility against men, need to be in control, calm under stress, fears and anger – it was always there to some degree. Following her discharge, Christy hung on to those problems, but transferred them to a civilian setting. The problems are with her still. "I change the locks on my house constantly," she claims. "I have great peripheral vision. When I'm in a crowd, I always sit in a corner. I know what's going on around me." A nervous, smiling woman, Christy chain-smokes and talks easily. She admits to self-mutilation, extreme depression ("I sleep a lot") and addictions, especially to shopping.

For Christy, the traumas of yesterday don't fade easily. She tries hard to forget them but explains, "PTSD is my movie. Whenever I start thinking about it, it doesn't stop." Because of the rape, she aligns her experiences more with POW's than with fellow vets; the rape was "deliberate, torturing and I couldn't get away." She occasionally has to justify her PTSD to fellow vets because she was not in actual combat.

In the late 1960's, Catherine trained pilots, ran a clothing store and worked with SEALS. It was during the Vietnam War. She was stationed state-side, even though she put in to go to Vietnam. Her bid was rejected. Her fiancee went instead and was killed in Laos.

"I was depressed when I first got out, mostly at the way vets were treated," she says. Particularly troublesome to Catherine were her memories of friends killed in a land so far away. And yet here on home soil, people were burning their draft cards. The memories of those deaths and the reactions of her countrymen have stuck with her to this day. "I still think about Vietnam all the time," she says. "I don't think I'll ever forget it."

Bobbie served as an enlisted Navy corpsman from 1964 to 1966 . She served her time entirely in the San Francisco Bay area, one of the hotbeds of anti-war sentiment.

Not only did anti-war sentiments fill the air, but the times were ripe with anti-female and anti-minority sentiments as well. A black woman in the service, Bobbie got hit from all directions. She describes a multitude of traumas, including the time she stood duty with a male soldier who pulled a gun on her when she refused his advances. "He never even got brought up on charges," she says.

Bobbie also describes feelings of helplessness in seeing young male friends, many of whom she trained with, going off to combat duty. "I knew of the high casualty rates," she says. "I felt helpless, that it should be me going."

And everywhere in the Bay area were those darn anti-war movements. Bobbie remembers protesters storming the gates of the base, picketing out front. Even after her discharge from the service, she remembers the extremeness of the times. The Black Panthers, the flower children, the Weathermen and the bomb threats – they were all present in San Francisco in the mid '60's to early '70's. And Bobbie experienced them all.

Bobbie's life after the service was no better. She got pregnant by a soldier who put in for Vietnam after he found out about the pregnancy; she delivered the baby, but gave it up for adoption. She then tried marriage, had another baby, got divorced, got married again and saw her husband murdered. From that point on, Bobbie went into hiding, bunkering up and becoming paranoid.

Bobbie summarizes the experiences and traumas of female veterans of all generations and situations. Traditionally not thrown into the actual battlefield, they fight a far more insidious battle:

Combat is a state of mind. It's a place I've never been, and can never leave. I didn't have to go halfway 'round the world to know what it's like to be in a combat zone.

SECONDARY PTSD AND MALE SPOUSES

As an official disorder, PTSD is new. How it affects veterans, male and female, and their significant others is still being researched. Like their male counterparts, women with PTSD have only recently drawn the attention of clinicians and researchers alike.

What is known about PTSD is that it affects significant others greatly. Male and female spouses, parents, children and other loved ones are impacted by the symptoms and behaviors of the disorder. Secondary PTSD is a factor for both males and females. According to an article in the *DAV Magazine*:[4]

Women (vets) who are divorced or separated, according to the National Vietnam Veterans Readjustment Study, have substantially higher rates of PTSD than those who are married, suggesting that PTSD has disrupted their relationships.

The spouse is most closely affected by PTSD in the home. Some clinicians cite their observations of the different reactions of male and female spouses. Psychotherapist Kathryn Berg has observed that "men who are partners of someone with PTSD tend to intensify their traditional male role." Males become captains of the ship. They tend "to take over, to manage, to fix it." Women partners, on the other hand, tend to become even more traditional and focus more and more on the relationship.[5]

Still other clinicians observe that male spouses do not stick around as long as females. Willing to put up with the disruptions of PTSD in the home for a little while, they eventually wear out. They split from the scene altogether. After all, isn't it the woman who's supposed to nurture everyone else? Why should the man of the house have to work all day plus put up with this crap?

Society's reactions to women with PTSD range from disgust to disbelief, further contributing to the traumas of female vets and their partners. Though eligible for PTSD treatment through the VA system, females often shy away from taking advantage of that treatment. The low numbers result in very few counseling groups available to female vets. It's a numbers game; because they don't show up, they don't enjoy the camaraderie and healing that's due them.

And so, female vets turn inward; they fight the war inside their heads and hearts, rather than seek appropriate help. Their war becomes their families' war, fought in the privacy of the home.

Male spouses who are vets themselves (especially those with PTSD) react differently than spouses who are not vets. The bond between warriors is applicable even when the warriors are husband and wife.

LIVING HAPPILY EVER AFTER, WITH PTSD

Catherine married when she got out of the service. After 10 years, she divorced her husband, blaming a lot of the couple's problems on herself and her troubled feelings about the war.

Eager to talk about Vietnam and the war raging inside her head, Catherine tried to open up to her husband. "It was too hard for him," she explains of their split. "He had never been in the service; he didn't want to hear about it." Catherine turned to veteran's organizations like the Vietnam Veterans of America and the American Legion for support. That worked, but her marriage to a non-vet did not. Today, she knows that the war and her years in the service played a bigger role in her marriage than she ever knew at the time.

Christy also got married right after the service. She married a fellow soldier, an infantryman. Her marriage was short-lived, however. After two years, Christy decided to leave her alcoholic, abusive husband. In the process of leaving, she found her tires slit and M16 shells right outside her door. She also found out that she was pregnant. Still, she was determined to start over. She split to another state and set up house in a new place.

Christy was determined to start her new life without a relationship. Her problems with men were insurmountable, she thought. There would never be anyone for her. Unable to shake the scars of rape and an abusive marriage, she put miles and miles between her and any guy she met.

But then she met Andy. They were hospitalized together at the VA. They started to talk and soon discovered the similarities of their stories. They married, bringing into the union Christy's young son and two bad cases of PTSD.

The marriage worked. "I relegated my needs to Andy," Christy admits, "because I felt it was my job to help him." She put her own PTSD on the back burner, partly because Andy had also become sick with cancer. Throughout their brief marriage (Andy is now deceased), the couple struggled particularly hard with Christy's problems with closeness. She kept her distance from everyone, including Andy and her own son.

Sam is Christy's 10-year-old son. He has the jumpiness of a child used to being around trauma, and the attitude of a kid headed for trouble. He uses the lingo of PTSD like an old-timer. He talks about his stepdad's startle reaction, and how he could never sneak up on him. He also talks about being "bad." His mother worries about his low self-esteem and his recent talk of suicide. She somewhat regrets the fact he knows far more than other boys his age. But maybe that's good, too, she reasons, because of the way the world is now.

Christy's extended family members have ignored her throughout the years. "Out of sight, out of mind," she figures. Her brothers and sisters feel awkward around her and show no interest in being involved in her life. But Christy bears no grudges. "They never experienced the major parts of my life," she says. "I only gave them outlines of what was going on." She also describes the strangeness of being away while they were growing up. "I still tend to think of them as they were back then. Little and young."

Though widowed, Christy feels she is finally on the road to recovery. The years she spent with Andy were healing ones. "With trauma, you can't accept it," she explains, "but you can adapt to it." She and Andy were well on their way to adapting to PTSD.

Christy continues her journey of adapting to PTSD on her own. She also fills her days with volunteer work. She's currently working on the issue of Agent Orange (which she blames for the death of her husband, several years her senior), and the struggles of women in the military. She pursues her causes with the passion and single-mindedness of a missionary.

Bobbie is also married to a fellow veteran. Both are Vietnam-era vets with active PTSD. Both fight the demons of the disorder each and every day.

Bobbie met her future husband, Mike, during a veterans' reunion. The two married a year later in the backyard of a Vietnam memorial. It was the perfect setting, she muses, for two souls lost in the war but saved by each other.

The couple shares the symptoms and behaviors of PTSD. Each deals with his or her own anger, sleeplessness, startle reaction, intimacy problems and depression, and each deals with the other's as well. "We are good for each other," Bobbie claims. "We watch each other's triggers, and we read each other well."

Mike is a survivor of multiple marriages. "When non-vets deal with vets who have issues, they don't get it," he explains. Though PTSD wreaks double havoc in their household, Mike still feels he is better off with a vet than with a non-vet. He credits the couple's survival with one simple fact: "I don't see Bobbie's issues as any less than mine." The two have developed coping strategies, both individually and with one another, that allow their PTSD problems to surface and be dealt with. There's no hiding of feelings, no stuffing away for another day, no pretending that all is well when it is not.

Sure, there are rough days. Mike describes the couple's occasional problems with intimacy, the days when Bobbie crawls into her PTSD shell and withdraws from him emotionally:

> *If your spouse is irritable, tending to show anger at the drop of a hat, you start to say, "I thought we had a good, loving relationship. And now you walk around with this cloud all day..."*

For her part, Bobbie is just happy that Mike has stuck around. All the men in her life have skipped out. "Where am I supposed to go when I'm hurting?" she asks. For now, she has Mike and the knowledge that he knows exactly where she's coming from.

CHAPTER FOURTEEN

WE WON THE BATTLE TODAY –
BUT HOW ARE WE DOING ON THE WAR?

PTSD AND COPING

Dear Journal,

Attended a support group for wives today. Felt pretty good when I left. Probably won't last. But maybe it will. Sure hope so.

Been readin' a lot about PTSD lately. Good to know why he does some of those crazy things. (Would be better if he didn't do them at all, of course.) But sure helps to know why he does.

Still get tired of explaining things to my mom and others. Don't think they'll ever get it. Oh well, who cares? I'm the only one who's gotta understand, anyway.

Feel sorry that he had to be in that dumb old war. But we've all been payin' for it a little too long. Time to move on.

Anyway, I like people, I like life and I like gettin' up in the morning!

Me (on the road to feelin' better!)

Coping with PTSD – an oxymoron? Is it really possible to live with the horrors of a disorder so unpredictable and so devastating?

Yes, say the experts, and yes, say the loved ones who have managed to live with it for so many years. And yes, they claim, it is possible to live with PTSD and be happy at the same time.

JUST SAY I WENT OVER THE HILL

Certainly one of the ways in which loved ones cope with PTSD is to leave it altogether. For some, the "other woman" – the memories of war – presents too formidable a foe. For them, the daily battles and stresses of PTSD are just too overwhelming.

That's what Cindy felt when she left her Vietnam vet husband after more than 20 years of marriage. Though she recognizes there were things she could have done to lessen the stresses, she says her decision to call it quits was the right one. The toll on her physical and emotional health was just too great a price to pay.

Barbara decided to leave her combat vet husband when the toll of PTSD fell mainly on her children. Both her adolescent son and her young daughter paid dearly for their stepfather's outbursts of anger, depression and erratic behavior. Barbara calls their son the "thermometer of the family, showing people what was really going on." He bore the brunt of the physical abuse which, as the thermometer, began to show in behaviors almost identical to his stepfather's. After nearly 10 years of marriage, Barbara decided that she and her children were through.

Some families choose a temporary separation instead of divorce. A temporary separation is not as final, and it gives everyone breathing space and think time. It's similar to the military concept of "stand-down," the respite before re-entering the hot zone:

Stand-down: A cessation of action, a time to repair, re-supply and refit prior to returning to action..[1]

Cheryl separated from her Vietnam vet husband following one of his many emotional outbursts. But this time it was different. Cheryl remembers the date clearly. It was Feb. 17, 1991. Her husband got up that morning, and started screaming, as usual, at the couple's young son. But today he added something new to the routine; today he began kicking wildly, at first in circles and than at Cheryl. She did her best to dodge the attack, but not before their son witnessed the entire ordeal. The young boy reacted with screams of "I hate you, Dad! I hate you, Dad!" Cheryl took the kids and left that morning and did not return for nine months.

The separation was beneficial for everyone. Everyone got a breather. Cheryl's husband went into intense therapy, Cheryl enjoyed quiet days of reflection and the couple's son and daughter had time to heal. The family reunited, boasting of greater solidarity and happiness than ever.

Children of vets with PTSD also weigh their choices. "Should I stay and help Mom? Should I get the hell out of here as fast as I can?" Ultimately, all children leave the nest; the timing of that departure often depends upon the ravages of PTSD.

Shannon recalls the many times she ran away from home to flee the violence of her vet father. She grew up with the fear of getting hurt. She remembers the strength of her dad's hands around her neck, choking her, and she remembers Dad beating up Mom. Today, she lives at home, more out of financial need than desire. But she also stays to protect her mom; she figures Dad's about to explode and lose it again, like he does every seven years or so.

Shannon's older brother left years ago, to get out of the house, everyone figures. He joined the service and got married. He and his wife are stationed several states away and appear to be doing well, far out of the reach of the family and its problems with PTSD.

Dr. Aphrodite Matsakis helps vets and their families face the effects of PTSD (or any other problem). She uses a simple approach in her clinical work with families. She poses this question: "What is your ability to love, work and play?" If the respondent claims to still have the ability to love, work and play – in spite of having PTSD – then Dr. Matsakis believes the situation is tolerable. The measure is not in the symptoms, she explains, but in the ability to accomplish those things in life.[2]

Dr. Matsakis is cautious about giving advice to spouses who are considering leaving the vet with PTSD. Ultimately, she believes, such a decision is always the individual's to make, not the clinician's. So many variables come into play including one's values, family pressures, societal expectations and support systems. Dr. Matsakis provides the following gauge:[3]

With the (spouse), the bottom line is life or death. If it's financial ruin, emotional ruin, physical ruin, if you're getting medical symptoms because you're doing so much for him or he's beating you – then you have to stop the giving. I won't ever tell a woman to leave. I only say you need to be safe – you need to go to a safe place.

The decision to stay with the vet or to leave is no easy choice. Spouses and loved ones who choose to stay do so for a variety of reasons. When the PTSD symptoms and behaviors are not severe, family life is not disrupted.

Life is tolerable, and family members make minor adjustments only. But when PTSD is severe, causing major upheavals in the home, the choice is tougher. The vet may need the support of his family, but those around him cannot tolerate the upheavals. Those who stay in this setting often do so out of moral or religious obligations. "I married for life, and that means in sickness and in health," they espouse. Or they stay for the sake of the kids or because they depend upon the vet financially. Still others stay out of fear; they fear what the vet will do, to himself or others, if they leave.

And sometimes simple hope is the reason for staying. Loved ones cling to the hope that things will get better and tomorrow will be brighter.

TOUGHING IT OUT: PERSONAL STRENGTH AND FAITH

Spouses, children and others who cope with PTSD invariably have some kind of inner strength, philosophy or faith that keeps them going. They speak of high self-esteem and a strong sense of self. They compare themselves to prisoners of war who have managed to stay positive and carry on even in the grimmest of situations. They refuse to assume blame for PTSD. Many credit prayer and faith in God for the ability to cope. (One wife asks, with every trying circumstance, "God, What do you want me to learn from this?") Others tell of taking one hour at a time, because PTSD changes so quickly.

Sarah has found her life with a Vietnam vet in constant turmoil for the past 10 years. The ups and the downs have been difficult to handle, particularly in combination with a full-time professional career. What has helped Sarah to cope, however, is an entire re-framing of life. She offers her philosophy in near poetic terms:

I used to think that my life would be orderly. I thought I would get up each day, go to a nice job and then come home. My house would be tidy, and my savings account would be secure.

But now I know, after living with PTSD and balancing all the things I have to balance, that life is not orderly. How could I have thought it would be, anyway? Life was never meant to be so sequential, it was never meant to be a straight path from point A to B. Instead, life is very ragged; the patterns of experience, including happy times and tragedies, weave in and out, throughout the years.

The only orderly thing in my life is that the sun rises each day, and it sets each night. Outside of that, life is very unpredictable.

No longer trying to control the variables in her life, especially her husband's PTSD, Sarah has settled in to a calmer existence. She claims to be happier with this new knowledge, and feels she helps her husband cope better as well.

However, Sarah warns, accepting life's chaos is not an excuse for becoming lazy and failing to plan for the future. "It does not mean that each day is a free-for-all," she says. "I do not get up each day and say, 'OK life, hit me with whatever you will.' On the contrary; I still live each day with a purpose and a plan. I still make lists and expect to accomplish certain things. But I now know that PTSD occasionally throws me a curve ball. I accept those curve balls, and move on. I adjust without falling apart, and hopefully I learn."

As natural to life as chaos are feelings of sadness and pain. It is especially natural for persons who have experienced trauma – for what is sadder and more painful than losing your friends in combat? Dr. Matsakis advises those who live around the vet to let him feel sad, and to let themselves feel sad or anxious or angry as well. After all, it's not easy to live with the aftermath. Dr. Matsakis further explains: "The wife, too, has to let her kids go through a certain amount of suffering, because suffering is part of life. It is a part of the human experience." Emotion without hurting one's self or others can be a sign of great progress.[4]

Accepting a certain amount of negative emotion may require a shift in the family's thinking, Dr. Matsakis continues. The family has to determine how much the children should be told about sadness and grieving and depression:[5]

> *Kids need to be told enough information so they don't blame themselves. Dad is sad because of things that happened in the war. Children can understand sadness, like their pet died. They might not be able to relate to the intensity of the emotion, but they can relate to almost anything emotional. They've also been angry, sad, cheated, happy.*
>
> *The wife mediates with children and extended family. She has to explain her husband to people. One way to do that is to create empathy. "Haven't you ever felt cheated, that you deserved the prize because you worked hard? Well, that's how Daddy feels." They (children) don't need to know all the details.*

Having seen a role model for expression of feelings, whether it be sadness or anger, children will know it's all right to express pain. "It's got to be all right to have emotional pain in a house instead of suppressing it," Dr. Matsakis continues. She warns, however, that children must be made aware that destructive anger is not acceptable.[6]

Shannon credits the pain and traumas of her childhood home for making her more resilient than others her age. Now a young woman in her twenties, Shannon has weathered the constant turmoil of her Vietnam vet father since birth. She bears endless scars. But out of the rubble has emerged something very good. Shannon credits PTSD with her own keen sense of the needs of others, and her respect for people. She particularly respects the veteran and his sacrifices: "Dad's taught me a lot about where I've come from and what the veteran did and why," she says. She is able to embrace new situations and new people with ease. She reserves judgment of others because, she explains, who knows what kind of journey their lives have been, what kind of roads they've traveled and what kind of pain they've endured along the way?

TOUGHING IT OUT: COPING SKILLS AND STRATEGIES

Besides personal philosophies, strengths and faiths, families tell of specific skills and strategies for coping with PTSD. Not all of the ideas will work for everyone; readers are encouraged to use the coping skills that work well for them and to consult professional clinicians.

LEARN ABOUT PTSD

Experts and family members alike praise the benefits of knowledge. What is PTSD? What can you expect from living with it? Who has it? As Fred Gusman, Director of the National Center for PTSD, Clinical Laboratory and Education Division, in Menlo Park, California says: "The more knowledge you have, the better equipped you are to understand it and look at how you're dealing with it."[7] Talking and listening to others (including the vet) about PTSD are among the greatest healers of all.

Though knowledge is usually more powerful than lack of it, some spouses do tell of feeling hopeless upon learning about PTSD. Initially they pray, "he's going through a phase, he'll get over it." But when they learn of the tenacity of PTSD, they panic. They are disheartened to know that the memories of trauma, though they fade over the years, never go away completely.

And yet, despite the harshness of a PTSD diagnosis, loved ones are better armed to live with it if they understand it.

OWN UP TO THE PROBLEM

For both the vet and his family, acceptance and ownership of PTSD is an important first step in learning how to cope with it. Psychotherapist Kathryn Berg says this ownership involves "taking responsibility for one's own PTSD or secondary PTSD, and a willingness to work on it." She elaborates:[8]

For the family and others, part of coping is taking responsibility for the choices about the effects (of PTSD) on our own selves ... We maybe can't do anything about the partner's limitation. But we can focus on ourselves – what limits we can set, what boundaries we can use for ourselves, how we focus on our own issues, our own self care, our own choices that we make.

Self-assessment goes right along with knowledge of PTSD in learning how to cope, says Fred Gusman. He encourages loved ones to ask difficult questions: "What are my issues? How have I been impacted by being in this relationship? How much of it is related to being in the relationship and how much has to do with the suitcase, or background, I bring to the marriage? How much is getting ignited by my partner's PTSD?"[9]

Gusman further explains that in any partnership including marriage, each individual brings his or her own suitcase of experiences to the table. Each has the responsibility of owning up to those experiences, so that together the couple can decide which ones to keep within the union. Assuming that PTSD would not be an asset, the person who brings it has the responsibility to deal with it (though not without the support of the partner, of course). Just like the spouse must deal with problems not desirable for the union (e.g., problems with money), so, too, must the vet deal with his own PTSD.[10]

Vets and their loved ones have the right to be happy, despite the vets' PTSD. Loved ones should not assume the responsibility or blame for war. However, they need to own up to their own issues as well as their own reactions to PTSD.

CARE FOR THE BODY AND SOUL

Whether indulging in small rewards like a quiet bath or taking major steps to reduce stress, persons who live with PTSD must take care of themselves.

It's hard, because loved ones are so used to revolving their lives around the vet. They relegate their needs to his, and they exhaust themselves trying to keep him happy. They take on added burdens, usually out of necessity, and face the rigors of everyday life alone.

But self-care is critical to the continued maintenance of the family. Loved ones must tend to their own physical, emotional, spiritual and social well-being. Some need to eat better or take a walk or keep a doctor's appointment. Others need to overhaul their lifestyle and find a system to deal with anxieties and re-distribute responsibilities. As Dr. Matsakis explains, getting into the problem-solving mode instead of the blaming mode is far healthier and more productive.[11]

Reducing and coping with stress is a big challenge. Stress-reducing ideas are the focus of classes, clinics and books available throughout the country. At its simplest, battling stress involves advice such as this, offered by a major hospital in the Minneapolis-St. Paul area:[12]

Some healthy ways to deal with stress:
- Talk things over with a friend.
- Do something physically active.
- Make time for the things you enjoy.
- Take a break from the situation.

Persons living with PTSD need to find their own ways to reduce stress and enjoy life. Exercising and finding time for friends (including non-vet friends, of course) are common prescriptions for good health. Others say they attend school, volunteer, express themselves through art, keep a diary or journal, or excel at work.

Some resort to more dramatic stress-reducing measures. They pursue an alternative lifestyle (e.g., live closer to nature, in the woods or on a mountain top), or follow a personal or cultural belief. Mike is a Vietnam vet married to Bobbie, a Vietnam-era vet. Both follow the Native American philosophy of "grounding" to deal with their own and each other's PTSD. Grounding involves coming to terms with one's problems through personal reflection. For

Mike and Bobbie, it involves respecting each other and allowing personal space.

Setting limits is an important stress reducer. Before divorcing her Vietnam vet husband, Cindy learned she had to set limits to the nonstop rotation of visitors to their home. What started as brief visits by vet friends turned into overnight or longer stays. Though Cindy never entirely convinced her husband of her need for privacy, she did negotiate occasional days and nights without intruders. She also set limits to what she would give to the marriage, putting those energies into her own well-being. She took adult extension classes and developed close personal friendships.

Others tell of setting different kinds of limits in their lives. One busy career woman tells of setting limits to the number of hours she works on the job. In so doing, she is able to free up more time for the intense needs of her Vietnam vet husband. "It's not easy to sit and listen to stories of Vietnam," she says, "when you should be preparing your budget sheets. But, he needs my attention and he needs me. I try to balance things out a bit more."

Whatever the pleasure or stress reducer, those who live with PTSD need to pursue it. Their own happiness, and that of their families, depends on their ability to stay well.

PICK YOUR BATTLES

In the early days of her husband's diagnosis of PTSD, Sarah took on a big job – alone. She decided that the world, at least her family, friends and neighbors, had to understand PTSD and had to accept it. Period. Not negotiable.

Sarah used every soapbox possible; she copied and sent literature about PTSD to others, attempted writing about it for publication, used family gatherings to tell her story, etc. But most of her efforts were in vain. Family members continued to question the validity of PTSD. The neighbors never did warm up to her. And the world – well, judgment is still out on that one.

Eventually, Sarah elected to pick her battles about PTSD much more carefully. Certain people need to understand it, she decided, and others were quite frankly not worth the effort. She stopped excusing her husband's behavior to others, and stopped compensating for his social shortcomings. She stepped off the soapbox and directed her energies towards living and coping instead. "Life is much easier," she says. "I still feel badly that people don't understand. I just think we're ahead of our time. Someday, the world will look a lot kinder on its warriors."

Sarah also learned to pick her own internal battles. She discarded the notion that she could fully understand PTSD and her husband's behaviors. She decided, instead, that PTSD is far too complex and far too unpredictable. She stopped analyzing her husband and stopped making him justify his every move. Relieved, Sarah went on with the business of living.

Mike, a Vietnam combat vet, believes that soapboxing about PTSD is a lot easier when done in a group. "Through such organizations as the Vietnam Veterans of America (VVA)," he explains, "we round over our sharp edges and square up society." Groups like the VVA not only help the vet to fit better into society, but also help society to become enlightened about PTSD and other veteran's issues.

COMPROMISE AND LIVE ALTERNATIVELY

Many persons who live with PTSD find their childhood images of romance and marriage crumble. The neatly trimmed house, the 2.5 children, the neighborhood picnics – all soon give way to reality. With PTSD, life often involves compromise. The wife who loves children decides not to have them because of the stress of her husband's PTSD; so she pursues volunteer work. The family that never gets invited to the neighborhood cookout decides to have its own party. Life is full of choices, and happiness is still within reach. Sure, you can't have it all with PTSD. But you can still be happy.

The wife of one combat vet describes how she managed to grab onto the happiness that eluded her for so long. For years, she grappled with the questions: Should I continue to work and leave my husband at home all day, alone? Should I quit work to keep him company? Should we hang on to the lakeside property because my husband loves it, even though I don't have time for it? Should we sell our home in the city because my husband hates the noise?

The questions tormented the woman for years until one day she stumbled upon the perfect solution. Driving in the country near her job, she spotted a big yellow house for sale; it was surrounded by 10 acres of unspoiled land and a beautiful pond. She couldn't wait to show her husband what she had found. He fell in love with it on sight. The couple sold their home and their lakeside property and moved in to the big yellow house.

But the move involved one other step. The woman insisted that the couple take in a boarder, a fellow Vietnam vet. The big yellow house could accommodate another person, she explained to her husband, and he could enjoy companionship while she worked. The arrangement was put in place, and three of them moved into their dream home together.

For her part, the wife says she got her perfect house and picket fence, though not quite in the manner she had once hoped:

> *A lot of people think I'm crazy to get into this arrangement. They ask me, "Why would you want to live with two vets with PTSD? Isn't one bad enough?" I explain to them that it is my only choice. My husband can't make it through the long days alone. The only time he feels better is with another vet – I can't help him, and I work. Anyway, should I give up being a part of life? Should I give up having a career and friends? Now that we have this big house, there's plenty of room for a third person. We couldn't have had a regular boarder, it wouldn't have worked with PTSD. But my husband's friend is the perfect person to have around. He understands my husband. In fact, the two help each other out during the day, and I'm not afraid to be gone any more. Life has never been so easy and never been so good.*

GET INVOLVED IN THE ISSUES

Alex is happy that his father has come to grips with his depression and shame over the war. A prisoner in World War II, the old man had belonged to an infantry division that history remembers as having given way to the Germans during a major battle.

It took years and years of soul-searching, therapy and history revisited to make Alex's father well again. Newer accounts of the battle are kinder to the men of the division; indeed, they had fought hard, and indeed they were not cowards.

This new account, coupled with involvement in veteran's issues, has given Alex's father a new lease on life. Today, the old man holds his head high; he eagerly participates in reunions of the old division and holds a leadership position. He is even proud of the role that he and his comrades played during the war. Alex, though not himself involved in the issues or greatly impacted by his father's PTSD, is relieved. He has supported his dad's involvement in the division and is always happy to lend an ear to exciting news about newcomers to the group.

Before Shirley got involved in the building of a Vietnam memorial in her home state, she felt alone in dealing with her son's PTSD. But work on the memorial brought her into close contact with others like her, others confused, scared and hurting.

Shirley enjoys many close friendships with other parents and spouses of vets. She is proud to say that many of her closest relationships are with the vets themselves. "They call me mom," she says; "they're all like my kids." Shirley penned a poem to describe the bond among those who worked on the memorial and share the experience of trauma:

> *The Meaning of the Red Ribbon*
> *It is on the left arm – closest to the heart for the bloodshed and the live blood still there in Vietnam.*
>
> *The tie is like the bond that pulled us together, gave us strength and courage to accept and respect ourselves. Made us secure to rise above the ridicule from the past.*
>
> *This Bond is like the Triune God we are on – as a mother and her newborn bond – so the people from the Vietnam Era have bonded.*
>
> *This bond is the one good thing to come from Vietnam.*

Shirley hates the Vietnam War and all its related issues, especially the POW situation, but is secure in her new friendships. She works tirelessly on behalf of veterans and feels great personal joy with each breakthrough. Tearfully, she tells of helping to get the remains of one POW brought back home.

Though war often takes the meaning out of life, some vets and their families find great purpose in working on behalf of veteran's issues. Through their labors, they rediscover that life really is important.

REMEMBER TO LAUGH

In the end, loved ones who successfully live with PTSD share the common ability to laugh in spite of it all. As Sarah explains, "With PTSD, a person could cry and cry all the time about all the problems it brings, and all the broken dreams of yesterday and tomorrow. But sometimes you just gotta sit down and laugh hysterically."

PTSD is indeed a dark comedy. The traumas and tears are overflowing. But there are funny and ironic aspects, too. Many loved ones are able to point out the hilarity of some of their moments.

The wife of one combat vet talks about being the only one in her large family to own a lake home. Her siblings eye her property jealously. "Isn't it a riot?" she asks. "I'm also the one who can't enjoy it; my husband's PTSD and panic attacks are so bad, we can't take the long trips to get there. You just can't have it all, can you?"

Another laughs at the daily traumas of getting her husband off to work. "I swear, if I didn't get up and lay his shoes and socks out, he wouldn't be able to get out the door." She shakes her head and chuckles.

THE VALUE OF TREATMENT AND SUPPORT

For both vets and their families, ownership and acceptance of PTSD should be followed by "education and support and peer connections about PTSD and secondary PTSD." So says psychotherapist Kathryn Berg, who, in her private clinical practice, works with families in crisis.[13]

Finding appropriate education, support and peer connections is not always easy, however, for either the vet or his loved ones. Family members claim to have an especially tough time finding help targeted at their special needs, both in learning how to assist the vet and how to cope with their own secondary PTSD. Begrudgingly, the wife of one combat vet says, "My husband's gotten a lot more support than I have."

Because PTSD takes such a terrible toll, families often begin their road to recovery by concentrating on the vet's needs first. A common cry is, "If he doesn't get some help, I'll go crazy!" PTSD resources for vets are found with the U.S. Department of Veterans Affairs (VA), which sponsors three types of PTSD programs: specialized inpatient PTSD programs; Vet Centers; and PTSD Clinical Teams. In addition, "a number of other support programs provide short-term inpatient treatment and aftercare, or address such PTSD related issues as ... homelessness. VA mental hygiene clinics and psychiatric wards, especially where no other PTSD program exists, also treat veterans suffering from PTSD" (*DAV Magazine*, January 1992).[14] Vets interested in inquiring about any one of these programs should consult their local directory assistance.

Many VA-sponsored vets' programs also include family components. As Fred Gusman explains, "if the victim of PTSD that we're treating has been living with somebody else, there has to be some residue." Confusion, anger, frustration and hurt are common feelings of the partner. "It does not do any good to treat just the veteran and not get involved in some sort of treatment process for the family."[15]

In addition to the public sector, more and more private therapists are being trained to diagnose and treat PTSD and secondary PTSD. Certainly, the private health field has a long ways to go in its understanding and embracing of PTSD. Further limiting the vet's access to private professional help is insurance; society is stingy in doling out money for mental health. Despite these problems, however, vets and their families can find clinicians who are trained in PTSD and who can be quite effective in dealing with it.

Peer support groups and networks provide yet another avenue for vets, who so often need to reach out to others in pain, and their loved ones, who find that the rest of the world just doesn't seem to understand. Even informal connections, such as the wife of a Vietnam combat vet talking to another, can mend spirits and save lives. One wife describes the value of peer connections in her life:

I long for my extended family – my mom, brothers and sisters – to understand what I'm going through. But they just don't get it. I feel so alone in my daily battles with PTSD. I put up pretenses when I talk with my family; I call them and they call me, and we all say that everything is fine. But it isn't. Some days I could just scream! And then I talk to another wife of a combat vet, and she knows exactly where I'm coming from. As we talk, it's as if she's nodding on the other end of the line.

Children and teens also benefit from support groups designed just for them. Like their adult counterparts, children and teens learn from each other. They also find comfort in the commonness of their stories and situations. Whether through support groups, individual therapy, or some other method, the important thing for children and teens is to "learn how to identify their feelings and needs and communicate them," explains Kathryn Berg, psychotherapist.[16] Other family members can also play an important role in helping children to put their thoughts into words, identify their feelings and even communicate more directly with the vet who has PTSD.

Often children and teens become adept, either through their own wiles or with the help of others, at figuring out how to focus on the things they can do together with the vet. They learn how to make the most out of what is possible. If Sally finds that Dad can't come to her soccer games because he hates crowds, for example, she can suggest the two take a long walk or make dinner together.

Formal treatment programs, peer groups, casual networks – these and other opportunities link vets and their families with valuable support systems. Talking, listening and sharing are important tools in the battle against PTSD.

COMPENSATION FOR THE PAIN

For many vets, the anguish of war takes away their ability to make a living. Depression, hypervigilance, sleeplessness – the symptoms and behaviors of PTSD do not complement gainful employment.

Service-connected disability ratings and compensation based on those ratings are available to veterans who qualify. Though many vets with PTSD claim that monetary compensation does not take away the ache or bring back their youth, they do say that it helps to ease the pressures and fears that go along with having no money – e.g., starving, being out on the street, being unable to provide for one's family. The compensation allows vets and their families to concentrate on what's really important: getting better.

The ratings are given through the U.S. Department of Veterans Affairs (VA). An application process is required, and the amount of financial compensation and benefits depend upon the percentage of disability granted, if any. Each state in the country has a Department of Veterans Affairs. In addition, many states have county veterans' offices, which can assist vets with their claims. Several vets' organizations have information and also assist vets with their claims. For information, call the U.S. Department of Veterans Affairs at their toll free number: 1-800-827-1000. (If the number has changed, check under the U.S. Government listings in your local phone directory.)

The National Vietnam Veterans Coalition Foundation is a "veterans created and veterans operated charitable organization dedicated to the betterment of our nation's veterans, their families and communities."[17] The coalition produces a booklet, *National Veterans Guide,* a handy listing of organizations (by state) helping vets and their families. The booklet includes the phone numbers to VA Regional Offices, VA Medical Centers and Clinics, Vet Centers, national cemeteries, the American Legion, the Disabled American Veterans and the Veterans of Foreign Wars. Vets and their families can get a free copy of the booklet (postage paid) by writing to:

National Vietnam Veterans Coalition Foundation
National Veterans Guide
1100 Connecticut Ave. NW, 12th Floor
Washington, D.C. 20036

VISIONS OF THE FUTURE

For a while, this sign could be seen on the bulletin board of one major PTSD treatment center:

Yesterday is but a dream,
and tomorrow is only a vision.
But today was a real bitch.

The sign is meaningful to both vets and their loved ones. For the events and traumas of yesterday are past, yet still with them; and tomorrow is so very far away. But today – oh, how tough the hours have been.

What will the hours, days and months bring for those who live and cope with PTSD? Will things really get brighter, or will everyone continue to live in such darkness? Loved ones themselves express doubt about the future. They say things like, "He isn't going to get over it; he's developed this kind of thinking pattern for too long." When many spouses and children, in fact, envision the next year or two, they see a future without the vet. He will kill himself, die of PTSD-related physical problems, leave the family or the family will leave him. And many vets share the pessimism. "PTSD is a death sentence," says one. "I read my medical reports and think to myself, 'That man is pretty messed up.'"

But the experts don't agree that all is bleak. Dr. Arthur Blank Jr. has worked with veterans and their families since 1973. Dr. Blank says:[18]

I think the long-term prognosis (of PTSD) is very good if people get adequate treatment and stay with it. Bad memories never go away completely, but most people can get to the point where they can have a decent life without the symptoms reappearing. Actually former POWs are a very good demonstration of that ... So having these symptoms doesn't necessarily mean you can't have a good life. It's a matter of getting them decreased in intensity and frequency.

Shirley, the spunky mother of a combat vet, agrees. She refuses to give in to the no-hope syndrome. She holds on to the belief that her son will win his battles with PTSD. "He's going to come back – he's going to come home like the rest of them. It's going to be a long, hard battle for him after 25 years on drugs." But still, he's coming home, and she plans to be there for the homecoming.

COMING HOME – WITH CONDITIONS

The vision of "coming home" lives boldly in the hearts of loved ones. Families dream of sharing the rest of their lives with the vet who is at peace with his past. The wife of one combat vet shares her very special vision:

Wife: God, will my husband ever be free of the haunting memories of war?

God: Yes, dear, the memories of war will fade – though they will never go away completely.

Wife: Will my husband ever look the way he did before going off to war? Will he be young and strong again?

God: No, dear, it is many years past. Your husband will still wear the wrinkles and stresses of time.

Wife: Well, will my husband still have nightmares? Will he still talk of taking his own life? Will he still get angry for no reason?

God: No, dear, the nightmares will lessen, he will no longer talk of taking his life and his anger will subside.

Wife: God, will we ever be happy again? Will we find that peace that has so eluded both of us?

God: Yes, dear, the answer to both questions is yes. You will both be able to get up in the morning and feel the joy of living and breathing. You will enjoy the scent of the morning, and the beauty of the skies.

But remember, dear, there are conditions to living with PTSD. There will be tough times ahead. Not every day will be joyful. There will be tears and there will be sorrow.

But through your pain and suffering, you will both be given the gift of a deeper secret and a deeper truth. The gift is yours alone to enjoy. You will share the knowledge that the experiences you have endured make you very, very special. And that life – despite its traumas – is indeed worth living.

ENDNOTES

INTRODUCTION

1. Many resources provide histories of PTSD. Nice summary written by Ken Scharnberg, "PTSD: The Hidden Casualties," *The American Legion* (January 1994), pp. 14, 16. Quick summary also appears in "PTSD: Treating the Trauma of War," *DAV Magazine* (January 1992), p. 8.
2. Scharnberg, p. 16.
3. Scharnberg, p. 16. Also cited by Jim Goodwin, *Readjustment Problems Among Vietnam Veterans*, Disabled American Veterans, National Headquarters, P.O. Box 14301, Cincinnati, OH 45250-0301, p. 6.
4. American Psychiatric Association, *Diagnostic and Statistical Manual of Mental Disorders, Fourth Edition,* Washington, D.C., American Psychiatric Association, 1994, p. 424.
5. Matsakis, Aphrodite, *I Can't Get Over It, A Handbook for Trauma Survivors*, New Harbinger Publications, 1992, p. xvi.
6. Matsakis, Aphrodite, personal interview, Maryland, Feb. 25, 1996.
7. Compiled from many sources including Scharnberg, p. 16; Goodwin, pp. 13-19; "PTSD: Treating the Trauma of War," p. 8.
8. Blank, Arthur S. Jr., personal interviews, Minneapolis, Minnesota, Feb. 6, 1996 and Feb. 9, 1996.
9. American Psychiatric Association, p. 425.
10. Cited in many sources including American Psychiatric Association, p. 424.
11. Wilson, John P., Cleveland State University, per correspondence, June 14, 1996.
12. Barton, Stephen, personal interview, Minneapolis, Minnesota, Feb. 12, 1996.
13. Blank, Arthur S. Jr., personal interviews, Minneapolis, Minnesota, Feb. 6, 1996 and Feb. 9, 1996.
14. Gusman, Fred, personal interview, Menlo Park, California, Feb. 21, 1996.

15. Ibid.
16. Ibid.
17. Goodwin, pp. 6-7.
18. Gusman, Fred, personal interview, Menlo Park, California, Feb. 21, 1996.
19. Goodwin, p. 10.
20. Blank, Arthur S. Jr., personal interviews, Minneapolis, Minnesota, Feb. 6, 1996 and Feb. 9, 1996.
21. Data cited by Goodwin, pp. 11-12; Scharnberg, p. 14; "PTSD: Treating the Trauma of War," p. 8; Matsakis, Apohrodite, *Vietnam Wives,* Woodbine House, 1988, p. 17.
22. Scharnberg, p. 18.
23. American Psychiatric Association, p. 426.
24. Scharnberg, p. 16.
25. Mason, Patience H. C., *Recovering from the War, A Woman's Guide* to *Helping Your Vietnam Vet, Your Family and Yourself,* Penguin Books, 1990, p. 218.
26. "Gulf War Triggers PTSD Increases," *The American Legion* (June 1992), p. 34.
27. Scharnberg, Ken, "They Aren't Just Rap Centers Anymore," *The American Legion* (April 1993), p. 28.

CHAPTER ONE

1. Matsakis, Aphrodite, *Vietnam Wives,* Woodbine House, 1988, p. xiii.
2. Dean, Chuck, *Making Peace with Your Past: Nam Vet*, Multnomah Books, Questar Publishers, 1988, p. 56.
3. Matsakis, Aphrodite, *Vietnam Wives*, Woodbine House, 1988, p. xv.
4. Dean, pp. 75-76.
5. Blank, Arthur S. Jr., personal interviews, Minneapolis, Minnesota, Feb. 6, 1996 and Feb. 9, 1996.
6. Berg, Kathryn R., personal interview, Mendota Heights, Minnesota, Feb. 6, 1996.
7. Ibid.
8. Gusman, Fred, personal interview, Menlo Park, California, Feb. 21, 1996.
9. Berg, Kathryn R., personal interview, Mendota Heights, Minnesota, Feb. 6, 1996.
10. Ibid.

11. Ibid.

CHAPTER TWO

1. Blank, Arthur S. Jr., personal interviews, Minneapolis, Minnesota, Feb. 6, 1996 and Feb. 9, 1996.

CHAPTER THREE

1. Berg, Kathryn R., personal interview, Mendota Heights, Minnesota, Feb. 6, 1996.
2. Gusman, Fred, personal interview, Menlo Park, California, Feb. 21, 1996.

CHAPTER FOUR

1. Berg, Kathryn R., personal interview, Mendota Heights, Minnesota, Feb. 6, 1996.
2. Matsakis, Aphrodite, personal interview, Maryland, Feb. 25, 1996.
3. Ibid.
4. Ibid.
5. Ibid.
6. Berg, Kathryn R., personal interview, Mendota Heights, Minnesota, Feb. 6, 1996.
7. Matsakis, Aphrodite, *Vietnam Wives*, Woodbine House, 1988, p. 76.
8. Barton, Stephen, personal interview, Minneapolis, Minnesota, Feb. 12, 1996.
9. Blank, Arthur S. Jr., personal interviews, Minneapolis, Minnesota, Feb. 6, 1996 and Feb. 9, 1996.
10. Barton, Stephen, personal interview, Minneapolis, Minnesota, Feb. 12, 1996.

CHAPTER FIVE

1. Ibid.
2. Ibid.
3. Drez, Ron, "Warriors," *The American Legion* (September 1995), p. 28.
4. Bille, Donald A., "Road to Recovery, Posttraumatic Stress Disorder: The Hidden Victim," *Journal of Psychosocial Nursing* (Volume 31, Number 9, 1993), p. 23.
5. Gusman, Fred, personal interview, Menlo Park, California, Feb. 21, 1996.
6. Berg, Kathryn R., personal interview, Mendota Heights, Minnesota, Feb. 6, 1996.

CHAPTER SIX

1. Mason, p. 264.
2. Matsakis, Aphrodite, *Vietnam Wives*, Woodbine House, 1988, p. 13.
3. Barton, Stephen, personal interview, Minneapolis, Minnesota, Feb. 12, 1996.
4. Ibid.
5. American Psychiatric Association, *Anxiety Disorders*, Washington, D.C., American Psychiatric Association, 1988, pp. 3-4.
6. Barton, Stephen, personal interview, Minneapolis, Minnesota, Feb. 12, 1996.
7. Ibid.
8. American Psychiatric Association, *Diagnostic and Statistical Manual of Mental Disorders, Fourth Edition*, Washington, D.C., American Psychiatric Association, 1994, p. 393.
9. U.S. Department of Health and Human Services, *Understanding Panic Disorder*, NIH publication number 93-3482 (January 1993, not copyrighted), p. 15.
10. Barton, Stephen, personal interview, Minneapolis, Minnesota, Feb. 12, 1996.
11. Berg, Kathryn R., personal interview, Mendota Heights, Minnesota, Feb. 6, 1996.
12. Ibid.

CHAPTER SEVEN

1. Blank, Arthur S. Jr., *Anger in Vietnam Veterans*, unpublished manuscript, Washington, D.C., DVA Readjustment Counseling Service (no date).
2. Berg, Kathryn R., personal interview, Mendota Heights, Minnesota, Feb. 6, 1996.
3. Blank, Arthur S. Jr., personal interviews, Minneapolis, Minnesota, Feb. 6, 1996 and Feb. 9, 1996.
4. Ibid.
5. Matsakis, Aphrodite, *Vietnam Wives*, Woodbine House, 1988, p. 133.
6. Mason, p. 263.

CHAPTER EIGHT

1. Blank, Arthur S. Jr., personal interviews, Minneapolis, Minnesota, Feb. 6, 1996 and Feb. 9, 1996.
2. Mason, p. 249.

CHAPTER NINE

1. Blank, Arthur S. Jr., personal interviews, Minneapolis, Minnesota, Feb. 6, 1996 and Feb. 9, 1996.
2. Gusman, Fred, personal interview, Menlo Park, California, Feb. 21, 1996.
3. Barton, Stephen, personal interview, Minneapolis, Minnesota, Feb. 12, 1996.
4. Berg, Kathryn R., personal interview, Mendota Heights, Minnesota, Feb. 6, 1996.
5. Ibid.
6. Barton, Stephen, personal interview, Minneapolis, Minnesota, Feb. 12, 1996.

CHAPTER TEN

1. Matsakis, Aphrodite, *I Can't Get Over It, A Handbook for Trauma Survivors*, New Harbinger Publications, 1992, p. 29.
2. Ibid.

CHAPTER ELEVEN

1. Matsakis, Aphrodite, *I Can't Get Over It, A Handbook for Trauma Survivors*, New Harbinger Publications, 1992, p. 35.
2. Mason, p. 243.
3. U.S. Department of Health and Human Services, *Understanding Panic Disorder*, p. 14.
4. Berg, Kathryn R., personal interview, Mendota Heights, Minnesota, Feb. 6, 1996.
5. Blank, Arthur S. Jr., personal interviews, Minneapolis, Minnesota, Feb. 6, 1996 and Feb. 9, 1996.
6. Berg, Kathryn R., personal interview, Mendota Heights, Minnesota, Feb. 6, 1996.
7. Matsakis, Aphrodite, *Vietnam Wives*, Woodbine House, 1988, p. 231.

CHAPTER TWELVE

1. Dean, p. 37.
2. "The Army of the Forgotten," *The American Legion* (June 1992), pp. 28-29.

CHAPTER THIRTEEN

1. Scharnberg, Ken, "PTSD: The Hidden Casualties," *The American Legion* (January 1994), p. 18.
2. "Women's PTSD Groups Surfacing," *DAV Magazine* (January 1992), p. 10.
3. Gusman, Fred, personal interview, Menlo Park, California, Feb. 21, 1996.

4. "Women's PTSD Groups Surfacing," p. 10.
5. Berg, Kathryn R., personal interview, Mendota Heights, Minnesota, Feb. 6, 1996.

CHAPTER FOURTEEN

1. Minnesota Stand-Down '93, unpublished newsletter (Volume One, Number Two, May 1993), p. 1.
2. Matsakis, Aphrodite, personal interview, Maryland, Feb. 25, 1996.
3. Ibid.
4. Ibid.
5. Ibid.
6. Ibid.
7. Gusman, Fred, personal interview, Menlo Park, California, Feb. 21, 1996.
8. Berg, Kathryn R., personal interview, Mendota Heights, Minnesota, Feb. 6, 1996.
9. Gusman, Fred, personal interview, Menlo Park, California, Feb. 21, 1996.
10. Ibid.
11. Matsakis, Aphrodite, personal interview, Maryland, Feb. 25, 1996.
12. "Some Healthy Ways to Deal with Stress," excerpted from a patients' booklet, Abbott Northwestern Hospital, Minneapolis, Minnesota (no date).
13. Berg, Kathryn R., personal interview, Mendota Heights, Minnesota, Feb. 6, 1996.
14. "PTSD: Treating the Trauma of War," p. 9.
15. Gusman, Fred, personal interview, Menlo Park, California, Feb. 21, 1996.
16. Berg, Kathryn R., personal interview, Mendota Heights, Minnesota, Feb. 6, 1996.
17. National Vietnam Veterans Coalition Foundation, *National Veterans Guide*, 1100 Connecticut Ave., 12th Floor, Washington, D.C. 20036 (updated 1997), p. 1.
18. Blank, Arthur S. Jr., personal interviews, Minneapolis, Minnesota, Feb. 6, 1996 and Feb. 9, 1996.

DIAGNOSTIC CRITERIA FOR 309.81 POSTTRAUMATIC STRESS DISORDER

Reprinted with permission from the Diagnostic and Statistical Manual of Mental Disorders, Fourth Edition. Copyright 1994 American Psychiatric Association

A. The person has been exposed to a traumatic event in which both of the following were present:

(1) the person experienced, witnessed, or was confronted with an event or events that involved actual or threatened death or serious injury, or a threat to the physical integrity of self or others
(2) the person's response involved intense fear, helplessness, or horror. **Note:** In children, this may be expressed instead by disorganized or agitated behavior

B. The traumatic event is persistently reexperienced in one (or more) of the following ways:

(1) recurrent and intrusive distressing recollections of the event, including images, thoughts, or perceptions. **Note:** In young children, repetitive play may occur in which themes or aspects of the trauma are expressed.
(2) recurrent distressing dreams of the event. **Note:** In children, there may be frightening dreams without recognizable content.
(3) acting or feeling as if the traumatic event were recurring (includes a sense of reliving the experience, illusions, hallucinations, and dissociative flashback episodes, including those that occur on awakening or when intoxicated). **Note:** In young children, trauma-specific reenactment may occur.

(4) intense psychological distress at exposure to internal or external cues that symbolize or resemble an aspect of the traumatic event
(5) physiological reactivity on exposure to internal or external cues that symbolize or resemble an aspect of the traumatic event

C. Persistent avoidance of stimuli associated with the trauma and numbing of general responsiveness (not present before the trauma), as indicated by three (or more) of the following:

(1) efforts to avoid thoughts, feelings, or conversations associated with the trauma
(2) efforts to avoid activities, places, or people that arouse recollections of the trauma
(3) inability to recall an important aspect of the trauma
(4) markedly diminished interest or participation in significant activities
(5) feeling of detachment or estrangement from others
(6) restricted range of affect (e.g., unable to have loving feelings)
(7) sense of foreshortened future (e.g., does not expect to have a career, marriage, children, or a normal life span)

D. Persistent symptoms of increased arousal (not present before the trauma), as indicated by two (or more) of the following:

(1) difficulty falling or staying asleep
(2) irritability or outbursts of anger
(3) difficulty concentrating
(4) hypervigilance
(5) exaggerated startle response

E. Duration of the disturbance (symptoms in Criteria B, C and D) is more than one month.

F. The disturbance causes clinically significant distress or impairment in social, occupational, or other important areas of functioning.

Specify if:
Acute: if duration of symptoms is less than three months

Chronic: If duration of symptoms is three months or more

Specify if:
With Delayed Onset: if onset of symptoms is at least six months after the stressor